AFRICAN TIGHTROPE

AFRICAN TIGHTROPE

*My Two Years as Nkrumah's
Chief of Staff*

Major-General H. T. Alexander

FREDERICK A. PRAEGER, *Publishers*
New York · Washington · London

FREDERICK A. PRAEGER, *Publishers*
111 Fourth Avenue, New York 3, N.Y., U.S.A.
77–79 Charlotte Street, London, W.1, England

Published in the United States of America in 1966
by Frederick A. Praeger, Inc., Publishers

Printed in Great Britain

CONTENTS

APPENDICES 129

ILLUSTRATIONS *facing page*

Foreword

Sir Robert H. Scott, GCMG, CBE

AFRICA is a land of such diversity and contrast that no two descriptions, by Africans or non-Africans, coincide. Accounts by foreigners, indeed, superimposed one on the other, produce the blurred effect of a composite photograph. It is only the snapshot taken by an individual observer which gives a sense of reality.

The strategic importance of Africa is underrated because strategy is equated with military strategy and expressed in terms of military power, trained men and advanced weaponry, in which Africa is weak. But strategy in a wider sense is concerned with external policy over the whole field: clashes of policy are more likely to manifest themselves in areas of instability than in areas of stability, in areas of military weakness rather than strength.

Imperial rule in tropical Africa created and left arbitrary and unnatural boundaries. Another legacy was the small size of the security forces, small because they were merely the local ancillaries. Imperial forces could always intervene if necessary.

For most of the new leaders of African states the problems of their armed forces were both unexpected and unwelcome. Unexpected, because in the pursuit of political power they had assumed that after independence neither internal security nor external defence would constitute grave threats; and unwelcome because they would have preferred to devote resources to social and economic ends. But in some cases the threats were soon found to be more serious than foreseen, and moreover armed forces became status symbols.

vii

Some, having resolved to increase their forces, found that this could be done only by relying on one particular section of the community, especially for the corps of officers. Such sections were not necessarily active political supporters of the party in power.

This is an aspect of government we are apt to overlook. We take for granted the advice given to the author by his predecessor in Ghana: the army must be kept out of politics and politics kept out of the army. To leaders of newly independent countries this is a perversion of reality. In 1964 Dr Nyerere put it in these terms:

> My duty was to ensure that I would not put my country into the hands of a single major power for military assis-tance. . . . There is always some element of risk about having an army at all in an under-developed country, but since you cannot do without an army in these times, the task is to ensure that the officers and men are inte-grated into the government and party so that they become no more of a risk than, say, the Civil Service.

With western and communist (and even some non-aligned) countries ready to outbid each other in the provision of weapons and training, it is not difficult for new states to diversify sources of equipment and methods of training. But the premium for political insurance is military inefficiency.

The author was Chief of Defence Staff in Ghana for twenty months, from January 1960 till his dismissal by President Nkrumah in September 1961. Though handicapped by lack of previous experience of tropical Africa, his snapshots of Ghana and the Congo illustrate the military problems of new states all the more vividly because of the strains imposed by Ghanaian inter-vention in the Congo: the desire of politicians to use the forces for political and prestige purposes, their ignorance of military administration, their haste, their suspicions.

The peace-keeping role of the United Nations is usually dis-cussed in theoretical terms. General Alexander's clinical history of the early phases of United Nations action in the Congo is written from the point of view of a soldier responsible for his men, expect-ing clear instructions on their task, impatient of the confusion in chains of command and of the lack of understanding shown by the United Nations of the way to form, support and employ mixed contingents in a country in a state of chaos.

When he went to Ghana, the author expected to spend two years quietly training the Ghanaian army to be an efficient force on a scale that met the country's security needs and at a cost that could be contained within the national budget; and he took it for granted that politics and the army would be kept apart.

Within six months he found himself leading a Ghanaian contingent into the Congo on an ill-defined mission, disarming mutinous and leaderless Congolese troops, and a centre of controversy in the Congo, in Ghana, and at the United Nations. He writes with some bitterness as he gives his own version of his actions—but the bitterness is tinged with nostalgia in his references to President Nkrumah.

August 1965

Introduction

WHEN I returned from Ghana on September 26, 1961, after just over twenty months as Chief of the Defence Staff to President Nkrumah, I met several people who said to me, 'You ought to write a book.'

Writing books is a favourite pastime of both serving and retired officers. Some are good and some are bad. Many of those written by retired officers are justifications of their past actions. Those by serving officers are usually more topical and a record of personal experiences in campaigns such as the Malayan Emergency. What a serving officer can write is restricted by the needs of security and the inadvisability of the particular officer's making enemies whilst still on the active list!

This book is certainly not written as a justification of any actions I myself have taken while serving in Ghana. I am writing it because I feel that it may be of interest for people to know the difficulties of a senior officer serving a newly independent African state, particularly when that country appears to be going more and more 'left'. Not many officers have been accused to their faces of being an 'imperialist', a 'neo-colonialist' and a 'communist'. I have had that variegated privilege. I have tried to avoid making unnecessarily unpleasant remarks about anybody. I like to remember the pleasant things which happened to me in Ghana rather than the unpleasant. There were plenty of the latter which I would like to forget. I think I can justly say that the months I have spent serving President Nkrumah were a great experience, and I hope that I myself, and those expatriate officers who served with me, now have a better understanding of the problems which these young countries face when they have to stand on their own feet. I hope also that possibly parts of this book may help some people in this country to have a better understanding of the problems which face the Commonwealth and the West in their approach to African problems.

Some of what is written is now outdated, because I could not publish the book before my retirement from the British Army in June 1965. Some of the opinions expressed have already been proved wrong—some have been proved right.

I should like to dedicate this book to the memory of the officers and men of the Ghanaian contingent who died serving the United Nations in the Congo. They were fine examples of all that is best in the Commonwealth soldier.

I

SERVICE IN GHANA

1 Off to Ghana

I RETURNED from Malaya in the autumn of 1957, having been nominated to attend the Imperial Defence College in 1958. It is the ambition of every army officer to go to the Imperial Defence College. It provides a chance to sit back and to broaden the outlook from the purely military field to that of wider world problems. From the point of view of an officer who has been a long time overseas, there is, of course, an additional advantage: the course is not too strenuous, and one is able to see more of the family than would be the case in any regular military appointment.

After leaving the Imperial Defence College, I went to the War Office for the first time in my life, working there in the Military Training Directorate and helping to start a branch which is now called Combat Development.

I had only been there approximately a year when I was approached and asked if I would volunteer for Ghana as Chief of Defence Staff to President Nkrumah. I knew that others had been approached on this subject and had declined. I do not know why I accepted and sometimes I think I was a fool to have done so. Various factors influenced me, among them pressure by the Military Secretary's Branch which by implication led me to believe that this might be my only chance of becoming a Major-General, the fact that I had never served in this part of Africa and was interested in a part of the world which seemed to be coming into the news to an increasing extent, and the money

3

incentive—the pay offered was very good. It also meant, of course, that I would be my own master to a far greater extent than had I stayed in the War Office.

There is no doubt that secondments of this nature were even then becoming less and less popular. There are several factors which contribute to this. One is the insecurity, as illustrated by the dismissal of officers from Ghana and now from Tanganyika. Another is the feeling that in the present day 'rat race' for jobs, an officer serving in an ex-colonial territory is apt to be forgotten, and a third, that whatever you do you are bound to be the loser in the end, because so few people understand the problems of officers serving African masters.

I am not quite certain why I finally wrote back to the Military Secretary agreeing to be considered for Ghana. I think it was because I thought that unless I did so I had only a very outside chance of ever reaching the rank of Major-General. Once there, it seemed to me that I would be able to soldier on until the education of my two elder children was completed. Anyway, I did accept, and in due course received word that President Nkrumah had accepted me and that I had been appointed.

When accepting the appointment, I did make the proviso that I did not wish to do it for more than two years, since I had been so much abroad both during and after the war, and I received a guarantee from the Military Secretary that he would do all things in his power to ensure that two years would be the length of my stay, although he could promise nothing. Unfortunately, Military Secretaries change, files are destroyed, memories are short, and shortly after I got to Ghana it was made clear to me that I might have to stay for three years.

On January 5, 1960, I flew to Ghana in a BOAC Britannia and was met on arrival by Victor Paley. His ideas of a hand-over were similar to those to which I have always subscribed. These are that the officer who is leaving the appointment is quite certain that nobody can do it as well as he can, and that the new arrival is only too keen to have the 'old man' out of the way. For these reasons, the handover was short and consisted of visits to President Nkrumah and the Governor General, attendance at the Accra Races, and finally a farewell parade to Victor Paley.

This parade was excellent. In his speech, Victor made the point: 'Keep the army out of politics, and politics out of the army.' It was a theme which I held to consistently in my advice to President Nkrumah, but I fear that this advice has now gone by the board and from now on appointments in the armed services may become more and more political. If Nkrumah survives his present crises, I am sure that he will eventually rue the day when he allowed politics to penetrate his armed forces. If, on the other hand, Nkrumah is overthrown, I am sure that Ghana as a whole will also rue the day when the armed forces were allowed to get mixed up in politics. At any rate, when I took over from Victor Paley there was no trace of politics influencing this sphere. The army consisted of three battalions and an armoured squadron. On paper, ambitious plans existed for the expansion of the army and the other two services. The air force was in its infancy, the Commander being an Indian and the Flying Training School run by the Israelis, an unhappy combination which I discuss in the next chapter. The navy was commanded by a retired British officer and had just acquired its first two ships, two minesweepers built in Britain.

Before settling to a story such as this, it might be helpful to provide some background to the position of Ghana in the African context, and a little about its history, climate, economy and the peoples that go to make up the country. The Gold Coast, as it was called prior to independence, was the first British colony in Africa to be granted self-government. This came in 1957 after a certain amount of trouble and considerable political agitation led by the Convention People's Party, of which Nkrumah had become the head. At that time, there were two main political parties in Ghana: the Convention People's Party, which in rough terms could be described as the left wing organisation and which, although it included several men of high standing, also contained agitators and rabble-rousers; the other party was the United Party, most of whose leaders are now in gaol. The more prominent personalities in this party were the intellectuals and moderates and many of the better-educated Ghanaians.

When Ghana obtained its independence in 1957, Nkrumah became the first prime minister; it was not until he decided to make the country into a republic in 1960 that Nkrumah assumed the title of President. Between 1957 and 1960 there was a Governor General, Lord Listowel. During this period a number

5

of United Party adherents defected to the Convention People's Party, usually for reasons of personal gain. One only has to read Nkrumah's books to realise that he is at heart a revolutionary. It has often been said that 'a leopard never changes its spots', and it must be hard for him to become the President and Father of a Nation so soon after being the left wing agitator. Much has been written, and he himself has said much about his anti-colonial and anti-Western political views, but the complexity of his character is illustrated by the fact that even when he screams anti-British slogans he still retains a number of Britishers close to him. For example, his secretary was a Miss Erica Powell, the Comptroller of his Household has been British until recently, and his Financial Adviser, Sir Robert Jackson, has only fairly recently left Ghana.

When the country obtained its independence, the economy was in a fairly sound state, the British having left a credit balance of approximately two hundred million pounds at the disposal of its new rulers. The annual revenue amounted to approximately £90 million—which is good for an African country of this size. However, the economy was largely based on cocoa, the production and sale of which was in private hands. Production still remains in the hands of the small Ghanaian farmer, but the marketing has now been taken over by the government and the price paid to the farmer is strictly controlled. The two hundred million pounds balance in the bank has almost all been spent—part wisely and part unwisely. The only other sources of income of any significance are gold and timber. The production of gold was in the hands of private British companies, all of which have now been bought out by the government except for the Ashanti Gold Fields, which are the most productive.

In size it is a small country, a little smaller than the United Kingdom, but climatically it can be divided roughly into three regions. The coastal plain is dry and hot with a fairly low rainfall; it is unproductive in the agricultural sense, and no mining areas exist. In the central region, that is mainly the Ashanti with Kumasi as its capital, the rainfall is much greater. The main cocoa crop is grown here. The north gradually merges into the desert; here, although the rainfall is heavy, it lasts for a very short time and the water soon disappears into the various rivers flowing south. This leaves the country very barren since irrigation systems are at present poor. The main source of livelihood for the people

6

in this area is growing tobacco for manufacture of locally produced cigarettes, and yams which are a staple diet of the
Ghanaian throughout Ghana.

Although Nkrumah has tried to break down the tribal
system, mainly by depriving the chiefs of their powers, there are
very distinct differences between the various tribes, even in a
country as small as Ghana, and these differences are much more
pronounced than those, say, between a man from Somerset and
one from Yorkshire. Most of the educated people come from the
coastal plain, the Ga of Accra, the Fanti of Cape Coast, and the
Ewe who live in the south-east corner of Ghana and many of
whom also live in Togoland.

The majority of good schools, both mission and state, are
situated in this coastal plain. This largely accounts for the higher
standard of education. It is also accounted for by the fact that the
two biggest towns of Accra and Takoradi, until now the main
seaport, lie in this area. A new seaport, Tema, has just been completed by British contractors, and a new town is being built,
partly by the British, partly by Italians and partly by Russians;
it is hoped that many light industries will be established there.
The Volta project, which is an immense irrigation scheme, will
also benefit the south in that it will, of course, have benefits for
other parts of Ghana. It is intended to use the power from the
Volta Dam, being built by American firms and largely financed
by America, to establish aluminium industries and provide power
for domestic consumption.

The Ashanti are the predominant tribe in the central,
cocoa-producing area, and such prosperity as does exist derives
from this crop. British policy did not allow foreigners to buy up
land and the small farmer still exists in large numbers, each producing a small crop of cocoa. From the point of view of pure
economics, cocoa production is not as efficient as it could have
been had it been organised by a large firm, such as Cadburys, but
it produces a living for a large number of independent-minded
people. The Ashanti have always been described as the warriors
of Ghana, but the Ghanaian as a whole is not a warlike person
and even this tribe does not seem to have retained many of its
traditional warlike qualities.

There is a sharp contrast between the inhabitants of the
southern and central regions and those of the north. There is also

7

a sharp contrast between the standard of living in the southern and the northern regions. In the north, glaring examples of malnutrition can still be seen, and women still work in the fields with nothing more elaborate for a dress than a leaf. The people still live in little mud-thatched houses and tribal affiliations are very strong. Although Nkrumah has done a lot to break down tribal jealousies, there is often very little love lost between the Ga and the Northerner.

Prior to the 1914–18 war, Ghana's eastern boundary was the Volta river, and the strip of land running north immediately east of this river was ruled by the Germans. This area has now been incorporated into Ghana as Trans-Volta. Like so many relics of colonial days, the eastern boundary of Trans-Volta separating it from Togoland is artificial, and the main tribe, the Ewe, is split into two. Since winning his fight for independence, Nkrumah's main battle cry has been African Unity. His local thoughts in this direction are concentrated on incorporating Togoland into Ghana and have taken concrete effect in the creation of the Ghana-Guinea-Mali Union. Unfortunately for Ghana, both Guinea and Mali are by far the poorer partners and any union of this kind can only be at the expense of Ghana. Such loans as Nkrumah has given or will give to either of these territories are unlikely ever to be repaid, and, in fact, the Ghana-Guinea-Mali Union really means very little.

Apart from the geographical disadvantages, such as the distance between Ghana and Guinea, both Mali and Guinea are former French territories whose common language is French, whereas the common language of Ghana is English. It is unfortunate for Nkrumah that he is surrounded by former French territories. His nearest ex-British neighbour is Nigeria, for which country he has no love. I believe that his dislike of Nigeria springs from the fact that he fears the latter will eventually take over the leadership in West Africa. This, of course, is logical since it is a far bigger country, in size, population and potential wealth, but it is not a pleasant prospect for a man who sees himself as the saviour of Africa.

African leaders often talk of 'African Unity' and pay lip service to a United Africa. It is, of course, far more likely that more countries than ever existed under the wicked colonialists will be created, since tribal loyalties are, by and large, much stronger than national loyalty. This is already becoming evident wherever independence is, or is about to be, granted. Quite apart from this, most African politicians tasting power for the first time like it, and they are most unlikely willingly to become a small fish in a big pool when they stand a chance of being a big fish in a little pool.

I think that the visitor to Ghana will be impressed by things other than those which he has read in the popular press. On first arrival you are struck by activity of all kinds, new buildings being erected, new roads, new factories and new projects such as the Volta. Whatever else may be his failures, this rapid modernisation of a former colony is due to the work of President Nkrumah. By devious means he has obtained the capital from both East and West. The traveller is struck also by the cheerfulness and laughter of the ordinary people, and the buxom mammies who rule the markets in their colourful costumes. Ghanaians like colour both in their dress and in their pageantry. There is no doubt that they are proud of their country, although some may be unhappy with many of Nkrumah's political statements and actions.

The most upsetting aspect to the visitor is the unnecessarily crude and stupid attacks on the West, levelled daily in the local press. This one tried to get used to, but it was not easy.

2   The Armed Services of Ghana

1. *The situation in early 1960*

AS I said earlier, prior to my arrival in Ghana I had very little knowledge of Africa and less of Ghana's armed forces. My first task, therefore, on arrival was to have a look at these. Some of what I say in subsequent paragraphs may seem critical of the period prior to early 1960, but the reasons for the state of affairs which existed at that time must be appreciated. At the end of the last war, many African soldiers who had given honourable service overseas returned to their countries, Ghana, Nigeria, etc., and the armies of these territories were reduced to semi-static forces, whose sole duty was to aid the civil power. As Britain was preparing to grant the West African territories their independence, it was natural that very little money should be spent on modern equipment for the armed forces. So far as the navy and air force were concerned, from the purely logical point of view there was very little reason for a small country like Ghana to have either. Nonetheless, in Ghana and in other new African states there is a burning desire for full status as a sovereign nation; still sensitive about their former colonial status, they want to have all the external trappings of independent nationhood, they want to be like 'other people'. Long established nations have armies, navies, and air forces. Ghana, then, must have them too. Prestige is all important and over-rides considerations of cold logic—the time required to build up an effective military corps, the cost of modern equipment, the economic weaknesses of the country, etc. It is hard to blame them for wanting to be like other people; but even their friends must deplore the impetuous, unthinking way in which Ghana's leaders sometimes rush their country into over-grandiose, uncoördinated schemes of military expansion. Dreams of an army, navy and air force second to none in Africa had been dreamt before my arrival, and Victor Paley had had quite a time preventing the Ghana government from spending a disproportionate amount of money on the armed forces. To a large extent he had succeeded, and when I arrived I found a state of affairs rather as follows.

The Police had practically completed rebuilding all their accommodation and therefore had good, new barracks throughout the country. The army had only one new barracks at Accra; most of the others were very old and dilapidated. A fair amount of money had been spent on re-designing the uniforms of the armed forces in order to get away from the colonial type dress, but very little had been spent on equipment and transport, with the result that most of it was worn out. For example, in one battalion, of the six 3″ mortars on establishment all but two were unserviceable, and in a mortar platoon I could find only one man who had fired his mortar within the last three years.

I came to Ghana with a completely fresh outlook. I had not served there during the colonial days, and once I realised the state of affairs I had to decide whether to take the Paley line of resisting expenditure, or moderate my attitude to fall in with the wishes of the Ghanaian government. A country such as Ghana enjoys only limited resources, both financial and in the technical skills of the individuals, and one had to strike a balance between the over-enthusiastic demands of the politicians and a minimum below which it was useless to argue. I therefore decided first to visit the main centres of armed forces training. To deal first with the army, the main army stations were in Accra, where there was the Armed Forces' Command Organisation, one Infantry Battalion and all the supporting services; an armoured squadron equipped with Saladin and Ferret armoured cars was also in the process of forming here. Just outside Accra, at Teshie, there was a training wing where such courses as Weapon Training Instruction, Physical Training and Minor Tactical Training were run. It was here also that Ghana was about to establish its Military

Academy to provide the basic training for potential officers. The course was to be of two years, very much on the lines of Sandhurst. I quickly realised that the pressure for Ghanaianisation would increase and I feared, in the event quite rightly, that the planned output of cadets, sixty a year, would not meet the political wishes of Nkrumah and some of his advisers, which were clearly to get rid of the British officer from executive position as soon as possible. I therefore decided that the size of the Academy should be doubled in order that more rapid Ghanaianisation would be possible. Naturally Nkrumah readily agreed to this recommendation and when I left the Academy was able to produce a minimum of 120 cadets each year.

Throughout my stay in Ghana there was this constant conflict between wishing to Ghanaianise rapidly and at the same time not wishing to see the efficiency of Ghana's armed forces deteriorate. The situation was complicated by the fact that Nkrumah wanted his army to be doubled and be given the best of modern equipment. He was also anxious that his air force should be created with great rapidity. New equipment and new aircraft require highly trained people to operate them, but it was very difficult to persuade the government that a pilot could not be trained to fly a jet in a year, particularly when people like the Russian ambassador would glibly tell Nkrumah that pilots could be fully trained in six months.

One of the lessons that I learned from my experiences in Ghana was that continual pressure to get rid of the British officers in a new independent state must be accepted. I felt that we had to face up to the fact that Pan-Africanism, coerced by anti-Western pressure groups, would force us to Africanise the efficient armed forces we have created in our colonial and ex-colonial territories, far more quickly than the orthodox soldier would like.

Amongst the papers Victor Paley had left behind him was a plan for the complete Ghanaianisation of the armed forces by 1970. Just before I was removed from Ghana I produced a plan for Ghanaianisation by the end of 1962. As things turned out, even that was not quick enough, although it meant a sharp fall in the efficiency of the country's armed forces. I felt that unless the British produce plans for rapid Africanisation in their colonial territories throughout Africa, we would experience a repetition of the situation which arose in September 1961, when all the

British officers in Ghana were summarily relieved of their commands; but it will have worse consequences, because in Ghana at least we had an Academy and were already turning out young officers in good numbers, whereas elsewhere in Africa it seems that the training of African officers has sometimes lagged.*

Apart from the building work necessary to double the size of the Military Academy and to provide a new barracks for the armoured squadrons, there seemed, on my arrival, little need for additional construction. However, as Nkrumah's plans for expanding his armed forces became more ambitious, we did in fact have to do a great deal more building in Accra.

The second big military centre was at Kumasi; it provided the basic training for recruits to all three armed services. There has never been any shortage of recruits. For one thing, the soldier had learned to trust his British officer, and for another, although a great deal of the accommodation had become dilapidated, by and large the Ghanaian serviceman was better off than his counterpart in civil life. The training centre was just big enough to cope with armed forces that were not going to expand, but I realised that if expansion was to take place it would have to double its output.

In the north is Tamale, the only northern town of any size, and here was stationed a battalion of Ghanaian infantry. The barracks were very old and required rebuilding. The fourth big armed forces centre is at the port of Takoradi, where in addition to an infantry battalion, there was at that time the nucleus of the Ghana navy, and it was planned to make Takoradi Airport the main air force station.

As I have indicated, Nkrumah very quickly made it clear to me that he wanted the army expanded rapidly. His ideas were by no means clear, partly because no civilian Ghanaian, and this includes Nkrumah himself, really understands the difference between a division and a company. After several talks with him, it seemed that he wanted a division of nine battalions, with full supporting arms, by 1964. I for my part made it clear to him throughout my stay that you really cannot have things both ways. You cannot Africanise an army which has in the past been equipped with nothing more complicated than a 3″ mortar, and at the same time issue it with armoured cars, guns, etc., and ex-

* Since this paragraph was written it has been shown to be a true forecast.

pand, unless you accept that the new equipment will be very badly maintained and the wastage rate extremely high. Unfortunately, Nkrumah did want it both ways. He wanted Africanisation and a modern army, both at the same time. I feel that in his heart of hearts he realised that I was right, and implied as much the evening he dismissed me, when he said that in order to get rid of the British officers he did not mind if the army was reduced to one battalion; but it was a very different story in early 1960.

I came to the conclusion that it was no good continuing to follow the Paley line of no expansion and no expenditure, but that one had to try to fulfil President Nkrumah's wishes, so far as this was practicable. I therefore made a plan which produced more or less one new battalion a year, together with the introduction of heavier, more modern equipment and adequate supporting services. Although this plan could hardly have been expected to produce much fruit by the middle of 1960, it was interesting to note that the Ghana army was far better organised to look after itself than any other contingent in the Congo.

Concurrently with the expansion and re-equipping, we decided to embark on a barracks rebuilding programme. Apart from any other reason, it seemed fairly obvious that at the present rate of expenditure the money available to the Ghanaian government was certain to get short sooner or later, and when everybody else was getting new houses and so many new projects were taking place in the country, it seemed only reasonable that the armed forces should take their share while they could.

Next to the air force. When I arrived in Ghana, the situation was, to say the least of it, an unhappy one. During 1959, two Indian air force officers had arrived to start planning the formation of the Ghana air force, and it was intended that the Indians should train it. Unfortunately, for reasons best known to the Ghana government, the establishment of a flying training school was entrusted to the Israelis. This Israeli training team took the form of a mission responsible to the Israeli ambassador and not under effective command of the Indians. In an infant air force, the flying training school is probably the most important wing and forms the foundation from which to build. Even if the Israeli officers and men sent to run the flying training school had been seconded in the normal way, it would have been complicated enough to keep harmony between two very dissimilar peoples in

14

running an air force, let alone the two of them keeping the peace with the Ghanaians. As very little progress had been made with the actual ordering of aircraft and the formation of the air force as such, I decided that the whole problem needed to be re-assessed. The first principle which I established with Nkrumah was that one country and one country only should be responsible for training. To my mind it could have been either the Indians complete or the Israelis complete. Nkrumah would not accept a solution of this kind, since he did not wish to offend one country whilst appearing to favour the other. I therefore, with great reluctance, suggested that as he had the British training both his army and his navy, the best way out of the quandary would appear to be to ask the British to take on the air force as well, asking both the Indians and Israelis to step down. In May of 1960 he agreed to this solution, which was put into effect—not, however, without a great deal of heart-burning and some cursing of General Alexander by both the Indians and the Israelis.

The only aircraft in the possession of the Ghana air force at this time were Hindustan trainers made in India, but the Indian air commodore had produced a very ambitious plan involving an initial expenditure of some £25 million. This envisaged the formation of two transport squadrons and two jet squadrons. It also involved the building of a large air base just outside Accra. My problem seemed to be to produce a more realistic plan costing less but still partially satisfying the ambitions of the President. An air force is of great prestige value in Africa. On their visits abroad, Nkrumah and his cabinet ministers had seen many expensive aeroplanes and watched flights of sophisticated jets. When discussing air force matters it was hard to keep them down to a sense of proportion. Other countries had large sophisticated aircraft and therefore as they were now an up and coming independent state, they themselves must have such aircraft. Some Africans are not easily satisfied with the argument that the type of aeroplane required in Africa is the short take-off transport aircraft, that no pilot, Ghanaian or otherwise, can fly a sophisticated jet fighter after three lessons, and that in any case such aeroplanes are very expensive to operate. Nor were they convinced by the argument that one squadron of sophisticated jets, even if acquired, can be of no possible operational value to the country. Again I had to produce a solution which was acceptable

15

to Nkrumah from the prestige point of view and at the same time was in some way related to realism. The plan which he eventually accepted was for Takoradi airport to be improved to house the training organisation and, in the long term, for an air base to be built at Tamale. The first operational aircraft bought for Ghana were light transport, short take-off aeroplanes, Beavers and Otters. These have now been followed up by the bigger Caribou, an ideal type of transport aircraft for operating off the many rough air-strips found in Africa. When I left, the tentative plan for jets was to order some in 1964—this, of course, being dependent upon the building of Tamale airport, on which work had not then been started. It is possible that the Russians have persuaded Nkrumah to have jet fighters earlier, but it would clearly be stupid to do so.

To my mind, the navy is the least valuable of Ghana's armed services. The army has proved itself by its operations in the Congo, the air force could be used for civil tasks, such as running flying doctor services and moving meat from northern Ghana, even if it is not required to take part in operations. On the other hand, Ghana can neither afford nor use a large, well-balanced, independent navy. A small force intended for anti-smuggling and patrol duties along the coast makes sense, but anything much more ambitious makes no sense unless it is co-ordinated with and deployed under a system of defence partnership with other countries with which Ghana has common interests. If, for example, the Commonwealth contains such common interests, Ghana's navy could be complementary to Commonwealth naval strategy. If a Pan-African partnership is desirable and possible for Ghana, her navy should be designed to be complementary to this. Ghana herself, on her own, cannot realistically pretend to splendid isolation as a mistress of the seas. The only ships in the possession of the Ghana navy in early 1960 were the two mine-sweepers built in Britain, but plans did exist for ordering further ships. During my stay, I did everything in my power to slow up the expansion of an armed service which I consider an unnecessary luxury, when there were so many other things Ghana needed.

It might be appropriate here to discuss the relationship between the Ghanaian and British officers. Although, of course, there were always exceptions, even up to the time of my departure

16

and, I assume, since, this relationship has, on the whole, been of the best. Little or no politics came into it and until Nkrumah succumbed to the various pressures which led to my dismissal, he himself subscribed to keeping the armed forces out of politics. As is natural with the educated in newly independent territories, the young Ghanaian officer dreamt of high rank at an early age. As we British officers made every possible effort to speed up Ghanaianisation, most of the Ghanaians realised that before very long they would obtain rapid promotion. This helped to produce harmony between the Ghanaian and British officers. There were, unfortunately, a few Ghanaian officers whose ambition outweighed loyalty to the armed forces, and they could now do a lot of harm; let us hope that they do not do so. The temptations to become anti-British and anti-white, even for a young officer trained at Sandhurst, are, of course, very great in the existing atmosphere in Ghana. On their travels they meet Nasser's men, they meet officers of Mali's and Guinea's armed forces, whose gibes about British generals and other imperialist commanders are insidious. It is greatly to the credit of the Ghanaian officer that, by and large, he did not succumb to this never-ending pressure. I fear that from now on these officers may be more and more forced to toe the line if they are to hope for further advancement. It is sad.

Whilst touching on politics, a mention might be made of the Ex-Servicemen's Union. At the beginning of 1960, there were two organisations which looked after the interests of Ghana's many ex-servicemen. The first was the Ghana Legion, a non-political body affiliated to the British Legion in this country; it runs villages for disabled ex-servicemen. The second was the Ex-Servicemen's Union, a body dominated by politics which played quite a part in the support of Nkrumah prior to Ghana's independence. At the beginning of 1960, Nkrumah saw the dangers of such an organisation and tried, by passing a law in parliament, to combine both bodies under the name of the Ghana Legion. Unfortunately, it now looks as if the old leaders of the Ex-Servicemen's Union have taken control, and I fear that the money allotted by the government to look after ex-servicemen is more likely to be used for political ends than to assist the needy.

So, early in 1960 the British officers in key positions throughout Ghana's armed forces were committed to planning rapid

17

Ghanaianisation together with a rapid expansion and re-equipment programme for the army, navy and air force.

2. *The Ghanaian Soldier and Officer*

Many people in this country are apt to judge Africans as a whole, and West Africans in particular, by the utterances and behaviour of their politicians. It must be remembered that out of the 6 million odd inhabitants of Ghana, probably no more than 10,000 are educated in the European sense of the word. Of these 10,000 many are confused in their ideas, having no background of educated parents to give them stability of thought, and are therefore full of theories culled mostly from left wing literature. The Ghanaian soldier belongs to the 'unsophisticated' majority. Those recruited in northern Ghana, who form about forty per cent of the army, have very little education and, until they join up, live near to starvation level. The clothing of their mothers and wives consists for the most part of a piece of foliage, replaced daily. Their allegiances have been to the local tribal chiefs. In spite of the efforts of the Convention People's Party to make a change, in northern Ghana the strength of the chiefs is still quite considerable. On paper they have been deprived of their authority, but traditional authority dies hard. The man recruited from this area is therefore simple, respectful, still holding to many of his tribal beliefs and suspicions. These men form the backbone of the infantry.

As one goes further south to the Ashanti and Ewe, Ga and Fanti, one finds the recruit better educated, in the sense that he has had more schooling and is regarded by the northerner as the 'spiv'. To call them spivs is unfair—most of them are delightful, cheerful men, but it is from amongst them that the barrack-room lawyer type, so well-known in the British army, tends to come. So far as the armed forces are concerned, the men from these tribes have sufficient education to be trained as specialists and technicians; the Ewe in particular, because in their area the mission schools have always been extremely good. It is too complicated a subject for the differences in make-up between the various tribes to be discussed in this context. I can only bring out the various characteristics of the Ghanaian serviceman which are common to all tribes—at least, as I saw it.

18

People are inclined to laugh at the old 'coaster's' love for the West African and find it hard to understand what makes many sad for Ghana at the moment and produces an urge to go back and try to help. They may laugh, but I grew to love the Ghanaian soldier, although I had never been to West Africa before and only stayed in Ghana for a comparatively short time. I believe it is true of any country to say that the soldier is a much better proposition to deal with than, for example, the politician, whatever the colour of the skin. I think it is because there is a bond between those in uniform that overrides all other differences, and the soldier, be he officer or man, realises that by and large those above and those below him are working for the good of the armed forces and not for the good of themselves.

The first quality which endeared the Ghanaian serviceman to me was that of trust. If you said to a group of men that you would do this or that—for example, build them a new barracks— they believed implicitly that you would do so. This had its snags, because if, in the event, you could not carry out whatever you had promised, the men became very upset and lost confidence in you completely. It was, therefore, very important never to promise the Ghanaian serviceman anything which you were not certain you could carry through, nor to tell him that something was going to happen which did not. Such mistakes nearly caused quite considerable trouble in the Congo, when units were told that they would be relieved on such-and-such a date, and, due to circumstances quite outside the control of whoever had given the promise, the date had to be postponed. I do not think that the Ghanaian soldier always trusted his senior NCOs, nor for that matter some of his own officers, but it was clear that the past behaviour of most of the many expatriate officers had taught him to place complete trust in the British officer. He possesses a lively sense of humour and on many occasions it has been possible to avert an ugly situation by making the men laugh, but one must be careful not to laugh at their expense. I was also impressed by the gentleness of the men. This gentleness, kindness and trust in their fellow men sometimes led them into trouble in the Congo. It was their trust in the word of the Congolese that they were their friends that contributed greatly to a disaster at Port Franqui and to the murder of the soldiers at the railway station in Kasai, which I describe later in this book.

19

Practically every facet of life in Ghana became more and more steeped in politics, but happily in the armed forces we were practically free from this taint until after my departure. I often argued this question with President Nkrumah, and, as the reader will recall, General Paley laid great stress on it. However, under the circumstances existing in Ghana, it always has been a difficult case to argue. The British argument is: 'Keep the army out of politics and politics out of the army—their loyalty should be to the President and to the state.' President Nkrumah's argument is that the Convention People's Party *is* the state; the President himself is loyal to the Convention People's Party, and therefore loyalty to the state means loyalty to the Convention People's Party. This was undoubtedly a point of view argued by many high members of the Convention People's Party. The danger of allowing army officers to get mixed up in politics is apt to be that some of them begin to think they could run the government better than the politicians in power, and as they have weapons they are in a rather strong position to translate such thoughts into practice.

Until quite recently, Ghana was blessed with the total absence of feeling over colour and race. Unfortunately, there are now some in high places who are definitely anti-white, and I believe that now there may be a few Ghanaian officers of a similar inclination. On the other hand, I never found any evidence of anti-white feeling amongst the men. I suppose they argued that they had always had a fair deal from the white officer, and nothing seemed to them to have changed this state of affairs. Although one or two British officers were beaten up during the mutiny of the third battalion at Tshiakiapa in the Congo, it was not because they were white but because they were close associates of the commanding officer, who happened to be Ghanaian.

The Ghanaians as a whole, and the Ghanaian soldier in particular, love pageantry. They love parades to meet the Queen, the President of Russia, President Sukarno of Indonesia, and do not seem to mind waiting for hours on the hot tarmac at Accra airport to have the pleasure of welcoming some visiting VIP. The soldier also likes his 'Durbar'. This is a meeting of the whole regiment or company, where men can put questions to the commanding officer or whoever happens to be the senior officer present, on any conceivable aspect of service life. The most com-

20

mon questions were about money. Like everyone else, the Ghanaian is always short of money—he is inclined to spend his pay almost as soon as he gets it and is keen to pursue any possible avenue by which he can collect some more.

Considering the background of many a Ghanaian soldier, straight from the 'bush' as one might say, the way he adapted himself to the almost impossible conditions existing in the Congo at the start, was amazing. The first battalion found themselves in a city, Leopoldville, more magnificent in appearance than anything they had ever seen in their lives, inhabited by people both black and white, behaving in a manner which they had never thought possible. The soldier found himself functioning, or trying to function, on orders which even a simple man knew to be ridiculous, and yet discipline held.

The Ghanaian makes a smart soldier and takes pride in his appearance. The standard of smartness was maintained in the Congo despite the appalling difficulties. In common with most Africans, the serviceman has a lust for learning, not only for himself but for his children, and one of his main concerns was to make sure that his children went to school. If, through mishandling, the selfishness of those above him, the emotionalism of Pan-Africanism running riot and the desire of some to please their master by putting into operation extensive plans which are clearly impracticable, Ghana's armed forces become more and more inefficient, those who will suffer will be the rank and file. They, least of all, deserve to suffer.

The small cadre of experienced Ghanaian officers carry a heavy responsibility, not only to their country, but to the men serving under them. Whatever else may have been said against the British officer, no one in Ghana can deny that he looked after the men and saw that they received fair treatment. History has shown that, in young countries, power is apt to go to the heads of the young, and there is a grave danger that this power may be abused. The sudden promotion to high rank very often spoils the best. It is all too easy to become a 'yes man' in order to hold on to the nice house, the car, the servants and the sense of importance which goes with them, and to forget the men. But I have good hopes that the majority of Ghanaian officers will come through these temptations with flying colours. The most important thing is that those at the very top should be prepared to sacrifice themselves, if this is necessary, for the good of the Ghanaian services, and I hope that the temptations may not prove too great for them. There is no doubt that, given a little more time, President Nkrumah could have had a thoroughly reliable, efficient corps of officers, but I am afraid that the political temptation to go too fast may rebound on the private soldier. Potentially, the Ghanaian officer has all the qualities which I have described as belonging to the soldier, but it will take a strong character to retain those qualities. However, one must not try always to judge standards of integrity and honesty in the same way as one judges them in a British officer. In Africa today some politicians do not always set the remainder of the population a very good example, and many are more concerned with the privileges of office than with the responsibilities.

Talking of 'temptations' makes me wonder what has happened to the Ordnance Depot. During the intensive building programme, many attractive items were stored in this depot, particularly such things as furniture and carpets. There was a cheerful, fat rogue of a parliamentary secretary who was continually trying to get the carpets out of the Ordnance Depot without payment. He was, naturally, stopped at the gate by the Ghanaian guard, who was supported in his action by the expatriate Depot commander. In the end, of course, this 'gross insult' from the expatriate towards a member of parliament was reported to me, and I had to smooth the troubled waters, but as far as I know he did not get his carpets. I wonder how many such carpets are left in the Ordnance Depot now.

Instances of this kind happened all too frequently, and I found myself repeatedly protecting expatriate officers from attacks, but usually they ended in laughter, and outwardly the Ghanaian concerned showed no ill-feeling. I suppose that the grudge could have been stored up, but I like to think that this was not the case.

The British armed forces have reason to be proud of the service given by their expatriate officers, some of whom still continue to serve Ghana as part of the British military mission. As officers in units, very few became involved in anti-British feeling or the political manœuvrings within the country. Those on the staff, however, were often subjected to accusations as false as they were hurtful, and it is to their credit that most of them kept their

22

heads and never lost their affection for the Ghanaian. It was a challenging task and I think everybody hoped that we would have been allowed to bring the training and organisation of Ghana's armed forces to a successful conclusion. This kept most people going. Of course, life had its compensations. The pay was good and many of the younger officers had far more responsibility than they would have had with the British army. The same applied in the newly formed Ghana air force.

3 President Nkrumah

MORE has been written about President Nkrumah, I should think, than about any other living African statesman. Views on his personality differ widely, opinions of his merits and defects are numerous, and the best way to handle him has been widely discussed. I knew Nkrumah for less than two years, but on the strength of the close working relationships I had with him I will try to give my impressions of the Nkrumah personality.

The first thing that should be made quite clear is the undoubted personal charm of Nkrumah. When interviewed in private he is charm itself—reasonable, polite and very friendly. This makes it difficult to assess fairly what goes on behind the façade of reasonableness, and it is undoubtedly his most powerful weapon. Also one must try to be fair in one's assessment and not be jaundiced by sad experience. On the surface and looking back over the history of Ghana since he took office, he would appear to be a strong man. Certainly, he is a dictator, but a dictator with a difference. Most dictators are bold, tyrannical men who have arrived in their positions through ruthless elimination of their opponents; Nkrumah obtained his prominence by leading agitation for independence and his gift for friendship enabled him to capture the leadership of his party. Only since he has come to power has he resorted to dictatorial methods for asserting his position: he will not hesitate to use the most ruthless methods and is prepared to be more extreme than the extremist to retain his own position and fight for the leadership in Africa.

24

If, as I have implied, he is not really a 'strong man', it may reasonably be asked how he has retained his position for so long? To understand this one has to understand the Ghanaian character. The average Ghanaian is a peace-loving person who abhors violence and loves pomp. Moreover, the vast majority are un-educated, unsophisticated people who are easily swayed by rabble-rousing tactics. Nkrumah understands these characteristics and plays on them. He now rules peace-loving people by fear. He gives the people plenty of pomp and ceremony, and retains in his cabinet rabble-rousers who can sway the crowd.

Like many in the African continent, he is a clever intriguer and his intrigue is calculated. He knows how to use people and how to play them off against one another. Unfortunately, he also finds it very hard to say no to anyone and to make up his mind. He is far too easily swayed by the last man he saw to be a really good dictator—good, that is, for his country. Because he has lost the support of most of the balanced intellectuals in Ghana—some he has imprisoned, some driven out of the country—he suffers from a serious lack of good advisers. He is far too ready to take advice which is best for Nkrumah rather than best for Ghana, and, because of his pre-eminence in the state, if he finds that what he wants to do is against the law, he is inclined to change the law. My experiences led me to the view that once he had made up his mind—or had it made up for him by the last person he had seen—it was best to act on his decision immediately, for fear he might discuss the subject with someone else and change his mind. If he had steeled himself to what he thought might be unwise or unpopular, he required action at once. Indeed, it was almost as if he realised he had this flaw in his character but could do nothing about it. He obviously did not like giving me the sack. When I came into the room, he was standing up. He was in a highly overwrought state and the one thing he wanted to do was to get this unpleasant business over and done with.

His English secretary was acutely conscious of Nkrumah's willingness to take advice not in the best interests of his country—or even of himself. Often she asked me to help him to do the wise thing—she truly believed him to be a good man, misled by bad advice. Nkrumah has a good deal of shrewd political sense, and when I was able to convince him that I was right he would willingly follow my advice. Before we left for New York in March

1961—he was to appear before the General Assembly of the United Nations—I helped prepare parts of his speech. I told him that all the other drafts, as they stood, would make him unpopular with many of the member delegations, and I sat up till four in the morning toning down the more virulent passages. Several of his advisers fought tooth and nail against the alterations I suggested, but Nkrumah realised that moderation was required. He over-ruled them, and in fact his speech was well received.

On other occasions, of course, I was not so successful; sometimes he would agree with me that something he had been advised to do was not really desirable and then go ahead and do it by some round about way. He would even make a decision that obviously concerned me—such as allowing the Russian military mission into the country—and not tell me about it, knowing full well that I would not approve and would do everything I could to talk him out of it.

Is Nkrumah a true communist? Perhaps he was inclined towards it in his youth, and even in the days when he was working to 'free' his country, but now he is an opportunist, using communist doctrine only when it suits his purpose and furthers his own aims. I fear that the Russians and the Ghanaian left wing may have been successful in persuading him that communist and Pan-African objectives in Africa are identical—a notable propaganda victory over the western powers. This means that in associating himself more and more with revolutionary movements in other parts of Africa, regardless of whether these territories are ruled by Africans or colonial powers, more and more he will appear to be following the communist line in his African policies. But his communism has never been very deep-seated. He still retains a love-hate relationship with the United Kingdom; hence his use for a long time of British officers and men in the training of his armed forces. He knew that from them he would get a non-doctrinaire, honest deal, whereas the communists mix doctrine with military training. On the other hand, he knows that the communists will co-operate in his endeavours and undermine his enemies—that is, all who frustrate him in his desire to be the most important African in Africa. I am sure that at heart he feels frustrated that he was born a Ghanaian. Ghana is a relatively small country, and does not really offer him enough scope for his grandiose ambitions. His aim is now—and has been for a long time—to lead the whole of Africa.

How far then does he genuinely believe in Pan-Africanism? I believe that he started on his road of leadership with a truly burning desire to see all Africa free from colonial rule, and that the Pan-African ideal is still his dominant motive. But I cannot really think that he himself believes half the things he says about colonialism and its opposition to a 'free' Africa. I remember dining one night at a state dinner given in honour of the Russian president, at which Nkrumah gave a virulent anti-imperialist, anti-British, anti-American speech. After dinner he came over to me and asked 'How did you enjoy my speech, General?' I replied that I found it somewhat painful. He then said: 'You must not worry, I had to please my guest.' Desire to please, but hardly responsible statesmanship by the president of a country, a member of the Commonwealth, speaking at a state dinner which was reported in the world press. Nevertheless, he does have a firm emotional attachment to Pan-Africanism—he genuinely believes in it and constantly works for it. I have called him an opportunist, but I think that his belief in Pan-Africanism does go deeper than this. Certainly, he wishes to be the leader of this united Africa but I believe he would rather forgo such a position than see the cause of Pan-Africanism collapse.

Does Nkrumah really believe in the Commonwealth? Although he plays an important part in its affairs and attends all the joint conferences of its prime ministers, I believe his attachment to the Commonwealth also is opportunist and retained for what he can get out of such membership. Commonwealth interests would always be sacrificed to those of Pan-Africanism and the retention of his own position. He is rather in the position of being a socialist and yet a member of the Carlton Club: it is convenient and comfortable to be a member although he will scarcely agree with the views of many other members. It makes him more respectable to be a member. But his speeches about imperialism and neo-colonialism are genuine in that he does believe that for economic reasons the West wishes to keep a strong hold on Africa; he also believes that Africans should be left free to run their own economic affairs, however badly. I wonder whether he realises that by following the Russian line he is in fact supporting just as big an imperialism as any in the western camp.

If, as I have implied, he is not the ideal man to lead Ghana through its present difficulties—difficulties chiefly of his own making—how does he last? He is cunning; he placates; he temporarily mollifies and you forgive him, but this does not stop him doing something worse the next time! He rules by fear a docile people and has few scruples. I do feel, however, that his golden days are gone. Of course he has his assets. The greatest of these is his complete freedom from colour prejudice. The colour of your skin, be it black, white, yellow or khaki, means nothing to him—in refreshing contrast to many other people of every colour. Secondly, he has a personal hold over a large number of people. His name still has great emotional appeal throughout Africa, because, for one thing, his country was the first of the British colonies in Africa to gain independence and also because he appears to have stood up to the major world powers and made an international name for himself as an African leader. But his influence throughout Africa must wane as more and more former colonies gain their independence. As far as the good of Ghana is concerned he has served his purpose: he has put Ghana on the map. But he is a revolutionary and he cannot stop trying to organise revolutions throughout Africa, when what Ghana wants is internal stability, good government, and financial sense. While I was in Ghana, I was constantly urging him to stop spending his money on grandiose prestige extravagances. I argued that the money would be better spent in building schools and training centres for Ghanaians, so that his own country would benefit. However my words had little long-term effect. Nkrumah is not a good administrator; he drives his financial advisers to distraction. He does not think in terms of the cost; if he wants something (such as a destroyer, because Nigeria has one) he wants it now and regardless of the state of the country's finances.

It is hard to predict future developments in Ghana. Undoubtedly the average Ghanaian is mystified and dismayed by present trends. Nkrumah is not a brave man and he is frightened—he is by nature an outgoing person who loves meeting people, but nowadays he keeps himself very much confined. Frightened men, clinging to power, egged on by other frightened but single-minded men, carry out extreme acts. Already there are many examples of such acts, and no number of Royal visits will, I fear, alter the trend. The hope for the future of the relationship of

Nkrumah and Ghana with the Commonwealth is that we continue to represent British policy fairly and vigorously to him, and trust that in time the effects of his triumphant tour of eastern Europe and the flattery accorded him there will wear off, although I am not entirely hopeful.

Despite all the difficulties, I would have tried to last out my term of office in Ghana, not only because of the sense of challenge, of not wanting to give up the battle, but also because I could not help liking Nkrumah. I wanted to help him to make the right decisions and to help save him from his bad advisers. If he were to come to me now and sit down and pour out all his troubles to me, I would do all I could to try to help him. He is a man betrayed by his own charm.

II

SERVICE
IN THE CONGO

4   The Congo Situation

SO much has been written concerning United Nations' handling of the Congo situation, the merits and demerits of the various Congolese leaders involved, and the attitude which the West and in particular Britain should or should not have adopted, that it is very difficult to avoid going back over ground which has already been covered *ad nauseam*. Nevertheless, it is true to say that the advent of the Congo crisis produced a fundamental change in Ghana's position *vis-à-vis* the West. Nkrumah's actions at the beginning of the crisis, and subsequently, were motivated by the hope that he could effect some form of union between the Congo and Ghana. They were also, of course, motivated by Pan-Africanism and anti-colonialism; but his primary aim was undoubtedly to bring about a union between the Congo and Ghana. It must not be forgotten that before the Congo obtained its 'freedom' President Nkrumah had played some part in bringing Kasavubu and Lumumba together, and for this reason he considered he had a good chance of obtaining Lumumba's agreement that Ghana and the Congo should be joined. The Ghana-Guinea-Mali Union no longer exists in fact or fiction, but, if one believes there ever was such a confederation, one could believe that the Ghana-Congo Union could become a fact. But, in truth, any form of union between Ghana and the Congo was more an emotional wish than a practical possibility. The obstacles to such a union are immense. To mention but a few: the Congo is vastly richer and bigger than Ghana; the population is approximately

33

three times as great; there is a language barrier and the Congolese people are entirely different in make-up to the Ghanaian.

I think it would be in place here if I described in outline what happened from my point of view, working as a moderate 'Ghanaian' trying to make common sense triumph over emotion. On July 5 the anti-Belgian riots broke out in the Congo, and on July 10 the Belgian army went into the Congo to rescue Belgian nationals. Lumumba at once appealed to the United Nations, and to Ghana in particular, to send forces to 'help eject the Belgians'. The Security Council did not approve Lumumba's appeal until July 13, but President Nkrumah had sent a mission to Leopoldville on July 12 to see what form of assistance Lumumba needed and whether it was desirable for Ghanaian soldiers to be sent. The size of the party sent was about six; the most important personalities in it were the ambassador-designate to the Congo—Andrew Djin—and the then Colonel Otu, the senior Ghanaian officer in the Ghana army. Ambassador Djin may be an excellent member of the Convention People's Party, the ruling party in Ghana, but, for a successful ambassador, he had several defects: defects which were not likely to assist him in giving good advice to President Nkrumah, who himself could have no conception of what was actually happening in the Congo. His main weaknesses appeared to me to be, firstly, he was anti-white—which coloured all his recommendations and activities—and secondly, he was so virulently anti-Belgian that it was impossible for him to see the rights and wrongs of an argument; thirdly, he did not speak French, which made it difficult for him to give direct advice to Lumumba and other Congolese politicians, and lastly, he quite failed to understand that troops placed under United Nations command cannot take orders from their parent country. This last defect caused a great deal of friction between him, myself and other senior Ghanaian officers. I think it is relevant here to mention that, whatever the rumours may have been concerning the action of the Ghanaian forces during their time in the Congo, there was in fact no occasion when they failed to obey United Nations orders as opposed to the conflicting orders which may have been issued either by the resident Ghanaian ambassador or direct from Accra. The second important personality in this mission, Colonel Otu, was to become Chief of Defence Staff of Ghana's armed forces. Otu is a pleasant man, good company and

34

a fair soldier, but obviously lacked experience. On this occasion he found himself facing a situation fit to daunt even the most experienced soldier, and he undoubtedly had a miserable and worrying time during his stay in the Congo. However, he survived and is still a serving soldier, which is more than I can say for myself!

This party took with them a radio transmitter, and the intention was that they should report back to Accra, primarily to recommend whether or not Ghanaian troops should be sent to the Congo. Although up to that time I had received no specific orders about the dispatch of troops, realising that neither Nkrumah nor his lieutenants understood what was involved in the dispatch of an 'expeditionary' force, I did alert two battalions to prepare to move to the Congo by air, should this be necessary. Earlier in this book I have mentioned the lack of preparedness of the Ghana army, and the thought of sending them off into the blue in this manner filled me with foreboding. Luckily I did have a certain number of very good British staff officers to help, and in Joe Michel, a Ghanaian who at that time was commanding the Second Battalion, we had a first class African soldier. I think my foreboding was justified, but their lack of preparedness turned out to be nothing in comparison with that of other contingents which were sent.

During the forty-eight hours after the departure of the mission very little information came through from them, and Nkrumah became restive. He therefore ordered me to proceed at once to the Congo to find out the situation more accurately, and to arrange for the dispatch of soldiers. He was determined to have the first troops on the spot, imagining that the Ghana army could on its own eject the Belgians and restore law and order throughout the Congo. Unfortunately, the Belgians at that time controlled the main airport at Leopoldville, which presented a snag to Ghanaians' landing there, and we did not appear to have in Ghana an aircraft with the range to make the trip. We tried, partly through the United Kingdom High Commission, to obtain permission for one to land at Leopoldville, but this permission was not forthcoming. As far as obtaining an aircraft was concerned, there was luckily an RAF Comet at Accra airport, which had brought out the RAF mission sent to prepare plans for the training of Ghana's own air force. President Nkrumah asked the

35

British government for permission to use this aircraft, and after some delay they agreed—the alternative being a Russian offer of an IL-18. Once permission to use the Comet had been obtained, I was prepared to take the chance about landing at Leopoldville, because as far as I knew the Belgians had no anti-aircraft equipment, and I hoped that if we could not land there it would be quite easy to divert to Brazzaville, just across the Congo river. In fact, when we took off we had not obtained permission to land at either airport.

For this reconnaissance I took with me a small party consisting, so far as I can recall, of Lieutenant-Colonel Malcolm Dewar as a spare officer, Major John Ewa, a very fine young Ghanaian staff officer who was at that time the senior Ghanaian intelligence officer, my ADC Captain Baddeley, a platoon commander and twenty-five other ranks. We took with us a high-powered wireless set so that I could send reports back to President Nkrumah. Before take-off we sent a message to Ambassador Djin, asking him to meet us at the airport.

The flight itself was uneventful, and night was beginning to fall when we eventually arrived over Leopoldville airport. After some argument the pilot received permission to land and was told to taxi to the control tower. He did so. Orders came through the control tower that no one was to disembark until a Belgian officer arrived at the aircraft. We waited. A gangway was put against the door of the aircraft, and I was ordered to disembark on my own. I told the other passengers, apart from John Ewa, to stay where they were, and disembarked. The Belgian officer was amazed to see a European general emerge from the Comet; he had expected an African. I was told that the rest of the passengers could disembark and remain in the hall under the control tower, but that they must consider themselves under arrest until I had seen the Belgian commander-in-chief, who happened to be present at the airport. I was then escorted to the commander-in-chief, who was in a highly excited state. He wanted to know on whose authority we were there. The only answer I could give him was that I had come on the authority of President Nkrumah who had received an appeal for assistance from Premier Lumumba. He was far from pleased with this answer. He then discoursed at some length on the atrocities which had been committed against Belgian women and children, and offered to show me some of

36

the women who were in an improvised ward on the airfield. I
declined to see these patients; I argued that as I was not a United
Nations official it would be better for these patients to wait until
somebody like Dr Bunche could see them, if he wished to do so.
There appeared to be no sign of the Ghanaian delegation, and it
later transpired that the Belgian military had stopped them coming to the airfield. I therefore felt rather at a loss and asked the
Belgian general if I could do anything to help until United
Nations forces arrived. He said I could do something at once. He
stated that the Congolese armed forces had been running wild in
Leopoldville and elsewhere. He had sent an ultimatum to the
commander of the Congolese troops in Leopoldville, saying that
unless they laid down their arms by midnight that night, he proposed to launch Belgian troops to disarm them. He considered
that as I represented Ghana, a country friendly to the Lumumba
regime, I could bring my good offices to bear to persuade the
Congolese troops to lay down their arms and thus prevent further
bloodshed.

It was now dark. I had never been in Leopoldville before,
nor had I met any of the Congolese personalities concerned. I
said I was quite willing to try if it would be of any assistance in
saving life, but that I had no idea how to contact the Congolese
authorities. For political reasons I thought it unwise for me to go
to the British embassy, and asked the Belgians if they could suggest any alternative. In an atmosphere of this nature many
African politicians thought that white men were either 'imperialist' or 'communist'. If you were British you were bound to be an
imperialist; therefore, if you were working for an African state,
it was most unwise to have overt contact with British officials,
however innocent this contact in fact might be, because it produced suspicion that you were engineering some imperialist
intrigue. The Belgian general suggested that I might go to the
American embassy, because the American ambassador, Timberlake, was fully in touch with the situation and could put me in
contact with anyone necessary. I agreed to do this, at the same
time asking whether anybody knew where I could contact the
Ghana mission. The Belgians promised that if the mission contacted them at the airport they would be told that I had gone to
the American embassy. It seemed to me that this was all I could
do if I was not to remain ineffectually at the airport. As the

37

situation was so confused I asked the Belgians to produce an officer to escort me to the American embassy, which they did.

We proceeded to the embassy through battalions of fierce-looking Belgian troops, but we did not see any Congolese soldiers. I arrived at the embassy and was seen immediately by Mr Timberlake—a man to whom I took an immediate liking. Subsequently I saw quite a lot of him unofficially, but it was very difficult to meet either him or the British ambassador without arousing suspicion from people like Djin and later Mr A. N. Welbeck, who succeeded Djin. I explained to Timberlake what the Belgians had asked me to do, and he gave his view that, if the Belgians attacked the Congolese in the middle of the night, this would confuse and aggravate the situation, probably leading to further bloodshed in places other than Leopoldville. He did not know whether the Congolese soldiers would agree to handing in their arms, because having thrown out all their Belgian officers they were now in a state of complete confusion, without rations and without leadership. He suggested that the best course was to ask the advice of the Belgian ambassador, who was still there, and of two ex-Belgian officers whom he could contact, after which I would have to contact Vice-Premier Gizenga and get his permission to go ahead. In the meantime, he would have a message sent to Djin to tell him where I was.

In due course the Belgian ambassador and the Belgian officers arrived; Dr Bunche came too, and when I told him what the position was, he said he would back me completely in my attempt to persuade the Congolese soldiers to hand in their weapons. He said that something had to be done to restore peace, at least in Leopoldville. The ex-Belgian officers thought there was some chance of success. The object was not to disarm the soldiers completely, but to persuade them to place their weapons in their armouries, where they could be kept and issued to those who needed them for duty. There is nothing disgraceful in this, and it is the normal procedure adopted by all disciplined armies. Subsequently this action of mine was misinterpreted to mean disarming completely the Congolese army, and political capital was made of it, even by some United Nations officials.

Eventually Mr Djin, Colonel Otu and, oddly enough, the Ghanaian ambassador in Moscow, arrived at the embassy. Djin was furious that I had contacted the American ambassador, the

servant of an 'imperial power', and all my explanations of why I
had done it were to no avail. I explained to him that as there was
no United Nations military commander in the Congo at the
moment, my actions would have to be agreed to by Dr Bunche as
well as by the Congolese government, since by now the appeal to
the United Nations had been approved by the Security Council
and Ghana could not act outside the United Nations. From start
to finish, Djin quite failed to recognise this fact, and it caused him
to regard me with considerable suspicion; but we agreed that
before I did any more about disarming the Congolese soldiers I
must get the approval of Vice-Premier Gizenga. Off we went to
get this approval from him. We found him in his house with a
Madame Blouin, reputedly a communist agent. He was in a state
of fear and readily agreed to my suggestion. I explained to him
that if this could be done there was much more chance of the
Belgians' agreeing to withdraw their troops from the streets of
Leopoldville. We decided that I would go to the main barracks at
about eight o'clock the following morning and address the
mutinous troops. Gizenga deputed his minister of Youth and
Sport, a delightful character called Mpolo, who was later murdered with Lumumba, to accompany me. I went back to the
Memling Hotel, where I was staying, to snatch a few hours'
sleep.

At eight o'clock next morning I met Mpolo in the hall of the
hotel, together with the two Belgian officers who had been at the
American embassy on the previous night. Mpolo objected to
the Belgian officers' accompanying us, because he said that this
would only antagonise the troops and deter rather than assist a
solution; they dropped out of the party.

As everybody knows, the world press was represented in
force in Leopoldville. Word had got around that we were going
to try to persuade the Congolese soldiers to hand in their arms,
and a small posse of pressmen pursued us to the barracks. It was
a queer feeling going down to the barracks, since I knew that all
the white officers had been ejected, and was not quite certain
what kind of reception an 'imperialist' general was likely to
receive. Mpolo seemed reasonably confident, but when we arrived
at the barrack square there seemed to be very few soldiers about.
With the assistance of a loud-speaker we persuaded about 2,500
men to come on parade, and I must say that they paraded very

efficiently in spite of their somewhat bizarre dress. Due to the Belgian departure the men were short of food, confused and thoroughly demoralised. Some had been out in the city, looting, but some must have just stayed in the barracks waiting for somebody to tell them what to do. Unfortunately, my French is not particularly good (this is an understatement), but luckily one of the reporters, de Borchgrave of the American magazine *Newsweek*, a very fluent French speaker, acted as my interpreter when I spoke to the troops. I inspected them to give me a chance to understand their mood. They seemed quite docile and I thought, therefore, that they would be prepared to listen. Mpolo had in the meantime organised a loud-speaker and a truck for us to stand on; he, de Borchgrave, myself and, I think, Colonel Otu, mounted the roof of this truck and addressed the troops.

I explained that we had come to the Congo as friends of the Congolese people to try to restore peace and tranquillity; that the Belgians would go just as soon as United Nations troops could take over from them—which would be quite soon—and that in the meantime it was important that people should keep their tempers and avoid further bloodshed. I explained also that the Belgians were in a nasty mood; that they wished to attack the Congolese troops—the last thing that either Ghana or the United Nations would want; that I had seen the Belgian commander the night before and he had agreed that if the Congolese soldiers handed their weapons in to their armouries he would call off any attack. I promised the troops that if they would agree to this I would leave a Ghanaian officer to supervise its execution, and go straight to the airport, to ensure that the Belgian troops stayed where they were and did not attack. Mpolo translated all this to the troops in Lingala, because many of them did not fully understand French, and de Borchgrave re-translated into French. We then asked all those who were in favour of handing in their weapons to shout their agreement. Without much hesitation there was a large shout, and we felt that we had achieved something.

As we had no radio or telephone communications with the Belgians, I then had to hurry off to the airport to persuade them to do nothing aggressive; otherwise the Congolese soldiers would feel I had let them down. On our way through we ran into a Congolese mob crowded round the body of a Congolese who had been shot. His murderer was a Portuguese who, on returning to

*Patrice Lumumba introduces the author to President
Kasavubu, July 1960.*

President Nkrumah, Marshal Tito and the author inspect a Ghana Army Guard of Honour.

President Nkrumah introduces the author to President Sukarno.

his house, had found the boy looting. To avoid a clash between the Belgian troops and Congolese civilians, we sent back to the barracks for an ambulance and a Congolese escort. With the removal of the body, the mob dispersed. It was rather enlightening, while talking to the mob, to find that they wanted to knife not the white man but poor Mpolo, the cabinet minister whom the ordinary man considered one of the people responsible for bringing all this misery upon them. My interpreter, a Ghanaian, just managed to stop an enthusiast from sticking a knife in Mpolo's back. After this little diversion we proceeded rapidly to the airport where I found Dr Bunche. I told him what had been achieved and asked him whether he would like to talk to the Belgian commander, to persuade him that the next step was for United Nations troops, as they arrived, to replace Belgians on the streets. Bunche replied that, as the Belgians had no official status in the country, he could not talk to them direct, but that I could talk to them and tell him the result of my conversations. Although in theory Bunche may have been correct, it seemed to me that you are very unlikely to produce results and make peace between two antagonists if you will talk to only one side.

However, I did talk with the Belgian commander. I found the Belgians just as suspicious and just as difficult as the Congolese. They were reluctant to bow to the inevitable—the withdrawal of their forces from Leopoldville—and it took me hours to get them to agree that United Nations troops, as they arrived, should take over from the Belgians, post by post—the actual take-over supervised by a United Nations officer, who for lack of anybody else was to be my ADC. When Djin heard that I had been talking to the Belgians again, he immediately accused me of co-operating with them—a further example of the atmosphere of suspicion and mistrust which ruled the day.

Next day the Tunisians started to arrive and, although they were somewhat reluctant to go on the streets at once, we did in fact start relieving the Belgians very shortly after their arrival. The situation, of course, was chaotic. There were no reception arrangements for the troops; we did not know where to house them; the Tunisians and other contingents arrived without rations, with no proper wireless communications, and some contingents arrived without any ammunition. There was no clear directive to the contingents to tell them what their powers and rights were, and what they could do in differing circumstances. Nor did many United Nations officers appear to think any directives necessary, but imagined that the mere presence of blue-helmeted soldiers would restore law and order. The Belgians had ruled by force; there is no doubt about that. The Congolese therefore understood force, and the United Nations soldier was discredited and abused as soon as the Congolese soldier discovered that United Nations soldiers had no power either to protect themselves or their companions. I will say more about this later in this chapter.

In the meantime I was sending regular reports to President Nkrumah, the gist of which was as follows: that any statements either by him or by any other African politician calculated to aggravate an already confused and difficult situation would be most unwise, and that he should support the dispatch of disciplined soldiers to restore law and order—not being too rigid about their being from Africa alone. In this respect I mentioned Gurkhas, Pakistanis and Indian troops as being highly suitable. I could well imagine that in the meantime Djin was sending quite contrary advice, but it seemed to me that until we got peace and tranquillity and prevented lawless bands of soldiers raping and shooting, it would be impossible to produce a viable political situation. I still think that my views were right.

The next problem that faced us was the Belgian desire to send soldiers into outlying places to rescue their nationals—the main centre of concern being Stanleyville. At that time, Lumumba was on a visit to Stanleyville and was known to have made several virulent verbal attacks on the Belgian people, calculated to incite the inhabitants against the whites who remained there—of whom there were still quite a number. The Belgian commander therefore wished to send some parachutists to Stanleyville to evacuate and protect the inhabitants. On the surface this would appear quite a reasonable request, but there were many other parts of the Congo where Europeans were unprotected and into which it was impossible to get Belgian soldiers. Whatever else the Congolese army lacked, it did not lack good communications, and once it became known that Belgian troops had arrived in Stanleyville, probably killing a few Congolese, I feared that reprisals would be taken against the Europeans in these outlying areas. I therefore suggested to the Belgian commander that I had

better visit Stanleyville myself to see Premier Lumumba before
we agreed to dispatch Belgian troops. With great reluctance he
agreed to wait until I had been to Stanleyville. The Americans
lent me an aircraft and away I went, my ears filled with reports
of the atrocities that were occurring in this city.

As I had already found for myself, most stories of atrocities
were exaggerated; I was therefore not unduly perturbed by the
reports coming from Stanleyville, but hoped that my complacency
was justified. We duly arrived at Stanleyville airport and taxied
to the control tower. The Belgian control tower officials were still
on duty but looked frightened. The airport itself was guarded by
gendarmerie who wore red bands upon their helmets; they are
the tough, long-service soldiers of the Congo. De Borchgrave had
managed to get on the aircraft and he helped me to explain to
the gendarmerie that I wanted to see Premier Lumumba.
Luckily, or not luckily, Djin was with Lumumba. The gendarmerie agreed to take me to the provincial President's House
where Lumumba was staying. Outside the airport gates there was
a crowd of frightened Belgians who seemed delighted to see us.
On arrival at the Presidential House, a lovely bungalow standing
on the banks of the Congo river, we found no sign of Lumumba.
A charming Congolese lady explained to us that he was the other
side of the river addressing a rally, and she did not know when he
would return.

There seemed no point in hanging about waiting for him—
the important thing was to find out what the situation really was
in Stanleyville. Someone had given me the name and address of a
Briton who was in charge of a tobacco factory, and I thought the
best thing was to try and find him; I asked the gendarmerie to
take me to the factory. Away we went, through streets deserted
except for occasional fierce-looking soldiers standing on corners,
and arrived at the factory. It seemed deserted, but eventually two
Belgians put their heads out of the windows of their flats and told
us where we might find this British manager. On being asked
what the situation was, they said that they had not been seriously
molested, but had been confined to their houses. This looked
hopeful. It was now about a quarter to two, and by two o'clock,
having picked up the local Congolese military commander, we
arrived at the factory manager's house. He was in bed, as was
another European who was staying with him. We got him up and

43

asked for his summary of the situation. It was quite clear what he thought. He said that as soon as he could possibly get out he was going to do so, because within eighteen months the country would revert to 'bush'. He slept by day because by night he was raided by drunken Congolese soldiers who insisted on searching his house while he stood against a wall with his hands up. His factory was still working because he had been ordered to keep it working by the local authorities, but it would have to stop production soon because he had no money to pay his workers; the Congolese had no money to buy the cigarettes, and there was no transport to send the cigarettes out of Stanleyville. He thought that the arrival of Belgian troops in Stanleyville at that time would have been disastrous. Stanleyville is a big city, and as soon as it became known that Belgian troops had landed on the airport, attacks on isolated residents such as himself would break out.

I had already sent a signal to Leopoldville banning the dispatch of Belgian troops because I was afraid that the Belgian commander might act without my knowledge. We asked the Congolese commander to keep his soldiers under control (fond hope!) and he promised to do so. A fortnight earlier he had been a corporal and now was sporting the rank of colonel. It was amusing to find that my friend Mpolo was dressed as a colonel when I returned to Leopoldville. Flushed by his success with the Congolese army, he thought he had better join it. Not content with being a colonel, when he discovered that I was a general, he put general's insignia on his shoulders—which shows how rapid promotion can be if you really set about it the right way!

By four o'clock we had returned to the Presidential House and found that Lumumba had come back from his rally. Djin was furious with me for not waiting there to see Lumumba, and would not listen to my explanations. I had not met Lumumba before, and was interested to talk to him. He immediately told me that the United Nations had failed in that they had not ejected the Belgians. I tried to explain that the Security Council had only approved the dispatch of troops four days previously and that it took a little time to move soldiers about the world. Even so, Ethiopian troops were due to arrive in Stanleyville that evening—which I considered a remarkable achievement. Lumumba did not seem to consider it at all remarkable, and said

44

that he fully intended to scrap his appeal to the United Nations and appeal instead to the Soviet Union, who would produce massive assistance to eject the Belgians.

We decided to have a conference on this question. Again de Borchgrave acted as my interpreter. The conversation was really fantastic. We argued about the cold war, hot war, Spanish war, Spanish-type wars, the danger of committing yourself to anybody other than the United Nations—but to no avail. After three hours or so of conference, Lumumba came down firmly on the side of appealing to the Soviet Union and Kasavubu, who was present, assented—if somewhat reluctantly. Lumumba said that, since it was so late, he did not intend to return to Leopold-ville that night, but would send me ahead with a typed message for Dr Bunche, giving his and Kasavubu's decision. While it was being typed he offered me dinner. Over the meal he talked cheer-fully of the pros and cons of their decision, which I still argued was stupid—although Djin did not agree.

Eventually the letter was ready and away we went, having sent a message from the control tower asking if Dr Bunche could meet me at Leopoldville airport. Lumumba had asked me to arrange for an aircraft to pick him up the next morning so that he could preside at the cabinet meeting necessary to ratify the decision to appeal to Russia for assistance. Bunche decided that he would ask the cabinet to meet the following morning to repudi-ate this appeal, and it did not matter whether Lumumba was present or not, since he had taken this decision without consulting his cabinet. The next day the cabinet, by a large majority, over-ruled Lumumba. He arrived back in Leopoldville, furious.

Many things have been written about Lumumba by political experts and others, but I suppose as a serving soldier who has been embroiled in the Congo crisis I am entitled to my own opinion. It seems to me that there is at present in the Congo no single politician capable of running it as a fully unified country, and that the best that can be hoped for is a loose federation. Lumumba thought that he could run the country as a unified state. His only personal advantage appeared to be that he was non-tribal, whereas the majority of Congolese politicians still hold their tribal allegiances. He was an excitable, emotional, inex-perienced man, quite uncontrollable and completely unreliable.

A small story may illustrate what Bunche and the others had

45

to cope with in trying to deal with him as the prime minister of the Congo. One evening at the beginning of the crisis he sent for me and said that he was dissatisfied with the number of Belgian troops still on the streets. I explained that the United Nations troops were taking over post by post, but that until a sufficient number of them arrived, it would be unwise to denude the streets of Leopoldville completely of soldiers. He answered: 'That may be your view, General, but we have just passed a resolution in cabinet saying that unless all Belgian troops have withdrawn from Leopoldville by six o'clock this evening we will appeal to the Soviet Union.'

I asked him whether, if the Belgian troops did withdraw from the streets completely, he would take responsibility for law and order in Leopoldville. 'No', said Lumumba, 'that is a military problem.'

The situation was resolved by my looking at my watch and saying to the prime minister: 'You said that the troops should all be off the streets by six o'clock. You do of course know, Monsieur Lumumba, what the time is now?'

'No, I have no idea.'

'It is ten past six', I said.

Meanwhile, Nkrumah had decided to dispatch his third and last battalion to the Congo and to promote all his senior officers to higher rank. This general promotion was done without my knowledge, and while I was out of the country. This is the sort of cross you have to bear if you serve under these circumstances. I did manage to make sure that Michel became the brigade commander and that Otu became the senior liaison officer working with the Congolese. Unfortunately Michel was killed in an air crash in September 1961; although Nkrumah did not appear to trust him, he was to my mind head and shoulders above all other Ghanaian officers. His prime interest was the good of Ghana's armed services, not the good of Michel. He was moderate, balanced and had not allowed promotion to conquer reason. He is a great loss to Ghana in its present difficulties.

Patrice Lumumba is now gone, and I think that his importance was over-rated both by Pan-African enthusiasts and by his Western detractors. I could never really persuade President Nkrumah to advise restraint in his conversations with Lumumba. If he had been able to bring himself to do so, Nkrumah would have done a great service to the Congo and to the United Nations. I believe that many in the West became far too excited about Lumumba and appeared to work far too actively for his removal. It was inevitable that by his own actions Lumumba should have destroyed himself without any pushing by Britain or the United States, and the West would not have suffered from the odium of blame for his untimely death. All the same, one can say this in his favour—he was a patriot.

When I went to the Congo on President Nkrumah's orders, I was officially Chief of Defence Staff, Ghana. Unfortunately, because it took some days before a United Nations Force Commander was appointed, I found on my arrival that I was the senior military officer in the Congo and therefore *ipso facto* had to take some action outside my terms of reference if the situation was not to deteriorate beyond repair. Once General Van Horn arrived I was able to hand over all United Nations responsibilities to him. My continued presence in the Congo was therefore unnecessary and would probably have been an embarrassment to Van Horn.

After talking to Dr Bunche, it seemed that the best contribution I could make to the situation was to fly to New York and explain verbally to the United Nations secretariat the real problem in the Congo and emphasise force requirements. This I agreed to do subject to the United Nations obtaining the permission of President Nkrumah, which they undertook to do. Later I make what I hope are constructive suggestions for the improvement of United Nations effectiveness in a situation similar to the Congo. In this section I want very shortly to cover some of the points which I made when I arrived in New York.

It seemed to me that, at the start, the United Nations headquarters in New York failed to appreciate the differences in the Congo problem from tasks which the United Nations had tackled previously, such as truce supervision in the Gaza strip. There appeared to be no form of military planning cell in the United Nations secretariat which could plan and produce the type of military force required to bring peace to a country which had been reduced to chaos overnight. Nor did many seem to understand the immense size of the Congo and its great lack of communication facilities, road, rail and radio. The only effective

47

means of transportation in the country was by air and the country was at least adequately supplied with airstrips.

One military commander had been appointed, General Van Horn. It appeared to me that he was bound to get mixed up with political and policy arguments in Leopoldville and would have little time for coping with the military situation, which changed from day to day. For this reason I advocated the appointment of a purely military commander to work under General Van Horn. From the start, the number of troops required to bring peace and tranquillity to the Congo appeared to be under-estimated. This statement, of course, is a half truth, because even if the United Nations had fully appreciated the force requirement they would have been hard pressed to persuade member countries to produce sufficient forces without drawing on the major powers, which was politically inadvisable.

The administrative problem within the United Nations force is also much more complex than it is in a force drawn from one nation because eating habits, types of weapons, types of ammunition, types of transport, types of radio sets, etc., can all be different. In normal armies, commanders receive a directive before they leave on a specific operation and the troops receive clear orders on their role and powers once they arrive in the country. This was not the case in the Congo. Troops arrived, officers arrived, commanders arrived, and nobody knew quite what they were supposed to do. It also seemed to me that it would be impossible to produce a viable political situation unless somebody first laid out clearly what was to be done about the Congolese army, which was in a state of chaos.

The problem was indeed immense, and in time the United Nations secretariat and its headquarters in Leopoldville did much to rectify the initial shortcomings and weaknesses; but as in all deteriorating military situations, the requirement was for speed and, had a better conception of the problem existed in New York from the beginning, I believe that we might have produced a happier solution.

I deal more specifically with the question of the United Nations military operations later in the book. These few comments will serve as an introduction to some of the stories I tell which I hope illustrate the almost unbelievable situations with which United Nations soldiers and civilians had to cope.

Once I had left the Congo I had no official position in the United Nations set-up and my subsequent frequent visits were made either at the request of the United Nations or at the request of the Ghana government in order that I might deal with some problem facing the Ghana contingent in the Congo.

5   The Welbeck Affair

AS time went on the Ghanaians became more and more unpopular in the Congo. This was due to several factors. The
continual interference by Andrew Djin and, later on, by his
successor, Mr A. N. Welbeck, made us unpopular with the
moderate Congolese leaders. The stream of instructions which
President Nkrumah sent from Accra, both to his army and to
Djin, annoyed the United Nations headquarters, although as I
have said previously, the army did in fact obey United Nations
orders to the letter. The fact that Ghanaian doctors and other
specialists were sent to the Congo outside the auspices of the
United Nations caused further ill-feeling. In time, things reached
such a pitch that Djin, in his absence on a trip to Ghana, was
declared *persona non grata* and Welbeck was appointed in his
stead—a move that I discouraged at the time as being 'out of the
frying pan into the fire'. Welbeck, a member of the old guard of
the Convention People's Party, was certainly first class as a rabble
rouser. But he was certainly no diplomat. His only advantage in
that field was that he did speak good French. His main weakness
was that in the evenings at the various parties held at the Ghana
embassy, he talked too much and at times prejudiced peace
between Lumumba and Kasavubu—a thing which at one time
seemed a possibility. Finally, the time came when Welbeck himself was declared *persona non grata* and given forty-eight hours to
get out of the Congo. Colonel (now General) Mobutu stated
unequivocally that unless Welbeck left within forty-eight hours,
50

he would be ejected by force. On hearing this I at once went to see President Nkrumah and stressed to him that in my view Mobutu meant business and that Welbeck should be withdrawn. Nkrumah would not hear of this, and sent messages to Welbeck telling him to stay at his post, because Mobutu did not represent the legal government. A large contingent of Ghanaian police was still in Leopoldville. This party had been sent at the beginning of the crisis to co-operate with the local Congolese police, but due to the growing unpopularity of Ghana, their efforts were becoming less and less productive. The commissioner of police and the Ghanaian police officer in charge in Leopoldville had made repeated requests for this body of men to be withdrawn, because they no longer served any useful purpose. The United Nations headquarters were willing to let them go. As policemen, and under the existing United Nations orders, the men suffered many annoyances from the Congolese and had little right of retaliation. It seemed to me that it was only fair to them that they should be withdrawn. Again President Nkrumah was reluctant to agree to this, because, of course, it involved a loss of prestige.

After twenty-four hours had expired and the messages from Leopoldville indicated more and more clearly that Mobutu meant business, I again saw President Nkrumah. It was agreed that the following morning I should fly down to Leopoldville and see what I could do to solve the crisis, but again the President was insistent that Welbeck should stay. An IL-18 aircraft was to take me at ten o'clock the following morning, Welbeck's time limit expiring at two o'clock in the afternoon— which, of course, meant that I would arrive after the expiration of the time limit. This worried me considerably. I therefore sent a message to General Rikhye, Hammarskjold's military representative at the United Nations, who was on a visit to the Congo at the time, asking him to ensure Welbeck's safety until I arrived. I received a brief reply that he would do his best.

After a great deal of heart-searching, I decided that indeed the only solution was to get Welbeck out, because, even if the Congolese had agreed to his staying this time, more trouble would undoubtedly arise very quickly. In the evening I therefore went to see Adamafio, who was then secretary-general of the party and close to the President. I told Adamafio that to my

51

mind there were three courses: the first was for Welbeck to with-draw and Ghana cease to have ambassadorial representation for the time being; the second was for me to take a sensible Ghanaian civil servant down with me who would try to act as a moderating influence on Welbeck; the third was to replace Welbeck by this moderating influence. Adamafio said that he realised my quandary, but did not think that Nkrumah would agree to any solution other than the second. I said to him: 'You realise this puts me on a spot, because I do not believe I can carry out the President's orders?'

Adamafio replied: 'Yes, I realise that, General'—and I do not think he was sorry!

In a last despairing effort to get sense to prevail, I asked to see Nkrumah at eight o'clock the following morning, before I left by air at ten. He agreed to see me and I put these courses to him. He would go no further than agree that I should take with me an excellent Ghanaian called Richard Quarshie, whom he said I could leave with Welbeck to act as the moderating influence I seemed to regard as necessary.

So, there it was. I was very afraid that, in the event, I would have great difficulty in carrying out President Nkrumah's orders, but there was nothing for it but to go down to the Congo and hope that some twist of fate would turn the course of events in my favour. This was not to be.

I was seen off in the IL-18 by the President himself, and away we went—three of us travelling in luxury in this large air-liner. The Russian crew were the height of affability, and when we crossed the 'line' the pilot put on a beard and I was regaled with Russian champagne and caviar. This somewhat restored my confidence and when we landed at Leopoldville I was in a frame of mind to handle any awkward situation!

The first thing that happened was Mr Pongo's putting the Russian crew under arrest: I managed to arrange their release the next day to fly Welbeck out, but they spent a very uncom-fortable twelve hours incarcerated in their aircraft on a hot run-way. Pongo was an epileptic and at that time minister of the Interior. Steve Otu met me at the airport at about half-past four, local time. As we drove to the United Nations head-quarters I asked Steve what the form was. He said: 'Not good.' It appeared it was unsafe to wear Ghanaian insignia on your shoulder titles; anti-Ghanaian feeling was intense. A contingent of Tunisians, together with a small posse of Ghana police were guarding Welbeck's house, which was surrounded by Congolese soldiers, commanded by a Colonel Kokolo. As yet no firing had broken out, but the time had elapsed and there was a danger that shooting would start at any moment.

On my arrival at the United Nations local headquarters, I first of all tried to contact General Van Horn, the UN military commander, but he was nowhere to be found. I then tried to get to see Rikhye—Hammarskjold's military representative who was in Leopoldville at the time; he was in conference with some of the Congolese cabinet who were 'raising hell' about Welbeck's still being in Leopoldville. Rikhye was trying to persuade the Congolese to call off their soldiers, and to procure this he said that I had come to see Welbeck and that I would be informed of the necessity of removing the Ghanaian ambassador at the earliest. It was not until about half-past six that I was able to see Rikhye. In the meantime there was a sudden burst of firing from the direction of Welbeck's residence (also the Ghanaian embassy), and everything seemed to have been let loose. Verey lights, machine guns, rifles, etc., blazed away in the dark and it seemed clear to me that if Welbeck was not to have his throat slit and a lot of people killed, the sooner I put him on the IL-18 and sent him away, the better.

I sat down and wrote Nkrumah a signal telling him this, and telling him also that in my view the police detachment, which was now concentrated at the airport, should also be withdrawn. Rikhye and I decided to try and get in to Welbeck and extricate him. All our conversations took place in the United Nations operations room, from which I tried to contact Mobutu to ask him to call off his soldiers. His reply was that his duty was 'at his post'. His post appeared to be his private house, well away from the scene of action, but he promised to send me an officer to go with us to Welbeck's home and make sure that we got through unscathed. The officer did not materialise for about one hour. Every conceivable ambassador under the sun kept ringing up, some of them telling me in no uncertain terms that the sooner I got Welbeck out of it the better for all concerned. To some my reply was that if Mobutu was such a good chap they might bring their influence to bear on him to withdraw his soldiers. This request of mine did not bear any fruit that night however. It would have helped me enormously to have consulted the British ambassador in Leopoldville, to have been able to explain to him the quandary I was in. I decided, however, that it would be improper and ill-advised for me, as the military agent in Ghana, to make any formal contact with the British representative, because without any doubt at all this would have been interpreted in Ghana, in the Congo and elsewhere, as 'ganging up' of the imperialists against African interests. I already had enough to deal with without hanging this millstone round my neck which would have probably made it much more difficult to explain my actions when I did return to Ghana.

Eventually we set forth in convoy. A United Nations jeep flying a huge UN flag led the way; Rikhye, Quarshie and I followed in a big American car; there was an empty car to take Welbeck and his luggage; another jeep brought up the rear. Although we tried to get in from two directions, it soon became clear that each side considered that we were reinforcements for the other and a considerable amount of stick was fired in our direction. During one attempt we decided to stop and get into the ditch, turning out all lights. Unfortunately, every time we opened the door of our American car the interior lights went on, which produced another hail of bullets. On arrival in this particular ditch, I discovered that Richard Quarshie was missing and therefore went back to the car to find him. He was lying on the floor. Although I explained to him that an American car of this type was not bullet-proof, he said: 'General, I have never been under fire in my life, and I never wish to be under fire again, nor do I wish to move; I would sooner die here than cross the road.'

I therefore had no alternative but to leave him.

After our abortive attempts to get to Welbeck, we went to the hospital to see if any casualties had been brought in. There we saw several wounded and three bodies—one Tunisian and two Congolese, including Colonel Kokolo's body. Spent bullets were breaking the windows in the hospital and one of the surgeons appeared to have gone out of his mind; he was running around picking up bullets and showing them to everybody with a certain degree of glee—I am not sure why.

Before we left United Nations headquarters I had had

several telephone conversations with Welbeck—extraordinarily, the telephone was still working. Welbeck explained to me in no uncertain terms that unless I arrived pretty quickly he would be killed. My reply was that if I tried to get through I too would be killed, and I had no intention of allowing this unhappy event to take place if I could avoid it. My advice to him was to go into as safe a room as possible and to stay there until we arrived.

Soon after our visit to the hospital we adjourned to Rikhye's house; we decided, over large whiskies and soda, that nothing more could be done in the dark and that I would try to get in as soon as it was light. Richard Quarshie and I then returned to our hotel and I dismissed the Ghanaian liaison officer, Captain Peel of the Green Jackets, telling him to meet me at five in the morning. Quarshie was in a very distressed state and I decided not to take him on the next attempt to extract Welbeck, but to leave him peacefully in bed at the Memling Hotel, putting him on to the IL-18 with Welbeck when I had extracted the ambassador. This decision had an 'interesting' sequel.

At about five o'clock away we went again to Welbeck's house and this time a Congolese escort met us at United Nations headquarters. All firing had ceased and I could see from the window of the operations room that the Congolese troops were, in fact, withdrawing. Our drive to the Ghanaian embassy was quite uneventful. Peel and I entered the embassy grounds, met the Tunisian commander and then passed on into the embassy building to fetch Welbeck and a companion who had been with him all the time. It was quite obvious that Welbeck had had a job to keep up his courage, and he looked in a pretty sorry state. When I asked him whether he wished to go, he said: 'Yes, indeed, General.' So I said, 'Come along, we will take what luggage we can.'

Peel and I grabbed what bags we could carry and piled everything into the small Volkswagen in which we were travelling. As soon as Welbeck was safely in the Volkswagen and we had set forth, his courage returned and he told me the astonishing 'fact' that the Belgians had been firing mortars at the embassy from across the Congo river. Although I explained to him that the range and the difficulty in locating the target made this impossible, I am quite convinced that Welbeck believed this statement to be true.

55

Our drive to the airfield was uneventful and the Congolese captain in charge of the escort was very courteous. Unfortunately our troubles did not end when I had put Welbeck into the aeroplane. No sooner had he sat down than the Congolese captain demanded to have a word with him. I agreed that he could come to the door of the aircraft, but no further.

Conversation on these lines ensued:

'Mr Welbeck, what have you done with Colonel Kokolo?'

'Nothing.'

'Yes you have; you have eaten him, and I would like to tell you what we will do to you if you ever come back to the Congo. We will chop you into little pieces and we will eat you.'

End of conversation.

I then quietly guided Welbeck to his seat and told him to stay there. Before allowing the Ghanaian ambassador to get into the aircraft I had taken the precaution of asking him again whether he wished to leave. He said: 'Yes.'

'All right', I said, 'in that case sign this piece of paper'; and on the back of an envelope I wrote: 'I am leaving the Congo at my own request. I wish to go.'

Welbeck signed. This, it transpired, was a wise precaution on my part. I, of course, in my simplicity, thought that my troubles were over and told the Russian crew that all was set to go. No sooner had the engines started to run than an excited Mr Pongo rushed across the tarmac waving a piece of paper. He had two reasons why the IL-18 could not take off. First, the luggage had not been subject to customs examination; and second, Ghana owed the Congolese government £450 for landing fees due on previous aeroplanes. The luggage, therefore, had to be unloaded and the contents were found to be quite innocuous—partly because we had omitted to bring Welbeck's safe and a part of his luggage which, I think, contained money. On the way to the airport, Welbeck had pleaded with me to send someone back quickly to get the remainder of his luggage. The question of the £450 was not so simple, but with the help of the Tunisian major who was the senior officer at the airfield, we gradually quietened Pongo down. Pongo is now dead, and one must not damn the dead, but I must say he was very objectionable that morning. When things became very unpleasant, I decided to go to the bar for a glass of beer while nerves calmed

At Luluaburg: the author and Brigadier Joe Michel with the Congo Garrison Commander.

On Training, February 1960. L. to R.: Permanent Defence Secretary Teshue Mensah, Brigadier Todman, Minister of Defence Nylander, and the author.

At the United Nations: the Ghana Ambassador to the UN, Alex Quaison-Sackey, discusses the Congo crisis with the author.

An Imperialist joke? Minister Adamafio, the Dutch Ambassador to Ghana, and the author.

down a bit. Unfortunately, Pongo pursued me to the bar and after he had spat in my face I decided that the time had come for me to leave the airfield, having assured Pongo that his £450 would be sent by me once I arrived back in Ghana. At last the IL-18 was allowed to go, and I must say that I was pleased to see the plane take off and disappear.

I have said that my decision to leave Richard Quarshie peacefully in bed at the Memling Hotel had an interesting sequel. It had! I had fully expected him to meet me at the airfield and peaceably board the Russian aircraft; it did not turn out that way. In the middle of my argument with Pongo, the unhappy Quarshie suddenly arrived with two fierce Mobutu soldiers walking behind him. Their sub-machine guns were firmly planted in his back and it took me some little time to persuade them to release him, so that he could enter the aircraft with Welbeck. It transpired that he had been peacefully asleep in his bed when he was awakened by a group of Congolese soldiery searching for 'the Ghanaian communist'. They had brought him to the airfield under escort to make sure that he did not stay in the Congo as a replacement for Welbeck. At least, that was the story. Poor Quarshie understood sufficient French to realise that they were discussing whether or not they should shoot him as a reprisal for the death of Colonel Kokolo. So far as the Congo and a diplomatic career there were concerned, this was enough for Quarshie. Very shortly after this episode he left Ghana and the last news I heard of him was that he was studying law in London.

I felt that I now ought to return to United Nations head-quarters to report that Welbeck had gone, and to pay my respects to General Van Horn, whom I had not seen since the start of this episode. Jonathan Peel, the liaison officer, asked if he could go away and have a shave. I agreed and asked him at the same time to try to collect the remaining luggage from Welbeck's house. This was the last that any member of the United Nations was to see of Jonathan for forty-eight hours or so. As he sped on his way in his Volkswagen he suddenly came up against a Congolese road block. He stopped and, as he had unwisely left the Ghana insignia on his shoulder titles, he was arrested, taken to the barracks, beaten up and thrown into jail with a Tunisian. He can tell the story far better than I can, but apparently the

Tunisian was rather excitable, insisting on creating a noise and shouting. This did no good but merely meant that from time to time the Congolese sentry would come in and beat up both the Tunisian and Jonathan. It fortunately reached Mobutu's ears that a British officer was locked up. He had met Peel and I think he had liked him, and therefore ordered his immediate release, sent for him and gave him a large drink. He then instructed a Congolese sergeant to help Jonathan find his car. They returned to the location of the road block—no sign of the car. The sergeant concluded that it had been taken to the barracks and, unluckily for Jonathan, they went back there. He was immediately rearrested and spent another unhappy twenty-four hours in jail. Maybe this will teach young officers to shave in the morning, however early the hour!

When I got back to the United Nations headquarters there was no sign of Van Horn and, in spite of telephoning his house, I could not contact him, since he was apparently exhausted by the firing of the night before. In the meantime the Congolese in their anger had refused landing rights for RAF aircraft which were doing regular flights to Leopoldville, supplying the Ghanaian contingent. This put me on a bit of a spot since I had counted on returning to Ghana on this scheduled flight. The situation was solved by the United Nations arranging for the aircraft to land at Brazzaville and also for a helicopter to fly me across the river. The rumour was going about that Mobutu had ordered my arrest, so I was pleased to get into the helicopter and away from the mad-house of Leopoldville. My flight back to Accra was not a happy one; I had disobeyed Nkrumah's orders and this worried me. He was at that time on a visit to Bamako, the capital of Mali, and from the signals that I had seen coming in to United Nations headquarters, he was not best pleased with my conduct. I felt that, once I saw him, Nkrumah would probably understand that my action was the only possible course. But I realised that I was in for another sticky time.

I landed at Accra airport late at night and was met by members of the Presidential Commission, who demanded an immediate short briefing at the airport itself. I was, of course, by then very tired, but explained briefly why Welbeck had had to come out. Two interesting points came out during this brief conversation. Firstly, apparently Welbeck stated that the attack was organised by the British—more about that later—and, secondly, he maintained that he would have stayed had he known that the President wished him to do so—more about this later, also. I had an uncomfortable twelve hours waiting for Nkrumah's return, and, in spite of more signals to him and a visit by the commissioner of police to Bamako, he would not agree to the withdrawal of the police contingent, who were now in a sorry state—the Congolese had cut off their water supply.

At about six o'clock next evening the President's aircraft arrived back. As he emerged, he turned to me and said: 'General, what is all the trouble?'

'Sir, I had better come and see you at Flagstaff House. There is a meeting arranged for seven o'clock', I said.

The President agreed to have a meeting, but postponed it until eight o'clock. At eight, a full cabinet meeting took place at which I detailed the course of events leading to Welbeck's withdrawal, and produced the piece of paper showing that Welbeck himself wished to come out and was not forced to do so. This solved one argument, but did not solve the argument of the British having organised the attack on the embassy. Welbeck's story was that, throughout the afternoon prior to the attack, the British military attaché, a kilted officer, had been moving prominently about amongst the Congolese soldiers surrounding the embassy. I was not in a position to explain his presence, since I had not been there at the time, and had no idea what he could have been doing. I felt sure, of course, that there was a quite innocent explanation, but the situation was rather awkward. Later on I wrote a note to the British High Commissioner in Accra, saying that this had placed me in a difficult position, and although I appreciated that the British military attaché in Leopoldville had a perfect right to go where he liked without interference from any Ghanaian, could he be asked to be more tactful when British officers serving an African country were trying to tackle an awkward situation. The reply I received was amusing, and was certainly never shown to Nkrumah. The British officer had apparently been sent to the Ghanaian embassy by the British ambassador to report on what was happening. Whether this was necessary was questionable. He had stayed the night with General Mobutu because the latter had considered it unsafe for him to return to his own house, which was near the firing. The reason why he was with General Mobutu at all was because he was keeping a long-standing dinner engagement. I doubt whether this explanation would have gone down very well with President Nkrumah!

To return to the cabinet meeting, Nkrumah handled the situation with a nice sense of humour and, from my point of view, very fairly. He said: 'Now, look here; the General was under my orders, although he disobeyed them. He was therefore responsible to me and to me alone. You failed to send any of his signals from the Congo on to Bamako and therefore I did not know the situation. Had I received the General's signals I would have agreed to his actions and I would also have agreed to the withdrawal of the police—who may now be withdrawn. I understand, Boateng, that you have been the most critical of the General's conduct. In particular, you consider that a Ghanaian ambassador should still be in Leopoldville; that being the case I appoint you as Ghanaian ambassador in Leopoldville.'

The look on Boateng's face* had to be seen to be believed. But he was a skilled enough politician to be able to extricate himself from this type of situation. He sent his staff ahead, who were immediately arrested and spent an uncomfortable forty-eight hours in jail. Boateng himself never went to the Congo, nor, so far as I know, has he been since.

Thus ended 'The Welbeck Affair'. My personal record made at the time is printed as Appendix A.

* Mr Kwaku Boateng was then minister of the Interior.

6 Ghanaian Contingent

1. The Ghana Contingent in Kasai

AS political tension rose in Leopoldville and Ghana became more and more unpopular with the Congolese central government, United Nations military headquarters found it increasingly difficult to protect the Ghana contingent from unjust accusations that they were collaborating with the resident Ghanaian ambassador. Quite rightly, therefore, the United Nations commander decided that in the interests of the troops and to allay suspicion it would be better if the contingent were moved to some other part of the Congo. In any case, a change-round of contingents from time to time was only fair because, by and large, the amenities in a place like Leopoldville made life much more pleasant for the soldier than being stationed in some remote village in the interior.

After about six months in Leopoldville, therefore, the Ghana contingent as a whole was moved to Luluaburg, the capital of Kasai province, and the Ghana Brigade headquarters took charge of UN tasks in Kasai and the break-away province of South Kasai, ruled by the self-appointed 'King' Kalonji. Although Kasai is only a province of the Congo, in size it is bigger than Ghana, and communications are much more difficult because the roads are so bad. Geographically it is very important and was especially so at this particular time. The 2,500 or so Congolese troops stationed in Luluaburg owed

61

nominal allegiance to General Mobutu in Leopoldville. The Lulua are the numerically dominant tribe in Kasai they form the old aristocracy of the province. They had never been great supporters of education, since other tribesmen had worked for them and they had owned the land. In the southern part of Kasai, 'King' Kalonji, who had formed a small break-away province, ruled over the Baluba. In the past they had been the serfs, but because they had attended the mission schools and become educated, it was from this tribe that most of the clerks and educated technicians were produced. There are two main centres of mining in Kasai, one at Bakwakanga, the capital of South Kasai, and another smaller mining area at Tshiakiapa in the west of the province. In both areas were diamond mines owned by Union Minière. Before the Ghanaian contingent moved into this province, the main garrisons had been supplied by the Tunisians, supported by a small Liberian contingent. These two had found the problem of keeping law and order in such a large territory quite beyond them and when the Ghanaian contingent moved in the situation was fairly chaotic. In the overall picture of the Congo, Kasai owed its importance to the fact that the railway running from north to south of the country went through the centre of the province. Materials and goods going from the Leopoldville direction are sent by river boat to Port Franqui, where they are transhipped to the railway running right through to Elizabethville. All imports are moved by this railway, since the roads are too poor for the extensive use of heavy transport. Several difficult problems faced the Ghanaian contingent when it arrived. All tribes, large and small, wished to have access to this railway, which meant that feuds were being fought for control of the country through which the railway ran. The Bakwakanga and Tshiakiapa mining areas lie away from the railway. 'King' Kalonji and his Baluba wanted a footing astride the railway, which was really outside Kalonji territory. The various tribes were also trying to eject pockets of other tribesmen from their territories. This complicated the running of industries, such as the mining in Tshiakiapa, since without trained Baluba operators it was difficult to work the mines. Arms were pouring in to Kalonji, who had some Belgian officers on his staff together with mercenaries of mixed nationalities. The administrative machine had completely broken down, mission hospitals had closed, and medical supplies had ceased to enter the territory. In fact, chaos reigned.

Tshiakiapa provided a notable example of the general situation. When the Third Battalion of the Ghanaian army arrived there, the medical officer visited one of the two existing hospitals. The situation in this hospital was indescribable. Shortly before our arrival, a detachment of the Congolese army, looking for Baluba, had raided the hospital and had murdered many of the occupants. The medical officer found bodies, which were two weeks dead, lying in beds. The stench was frightful; all the staff had fled. Practically no medical supplies existed. The two main mines and the cotton mill had stopped working because Baluba were being murdered and dared not go to work. The Liberian contingent which had been there previously had established a refugee camp for Baluba, but the food supplies for them were totally inadequate. The United Nations' Food Relief unit had started to make strenuous efforts to relieve the famine in Kasai, but it was going to take some time to catch up with the need, and in Kalonji's territory the plight of refugees was worse even than in Tshiakiapa. The atmosphere of unreasonableness and mistrust between the various tribes is well illustrated by the difficulties which faced Colonel Hansen, commanding the Third Battalion.

If the economy of the whole area round Tshiakiapa was to be restored, it was essential to start the mines and factories working again. It was also essential to sow the crops if the following year the people were not to starve. The key to these problems lay in persuading the local Lulua authorities to let the Baluba work and to stop persecuting non-Lulua peoples who lived on the land. Colonel Hansen therefore called a meeting of the Lulua chiefs. The palaver was most impressive, and he was presented with a tiger skin to show the chiefs' respect. Colonel Hansen explained the necessity for allowing the Baluba to work and his explanation was received with many nods. The leading chief then made a speech, the gist of which was that they all agreed with the Ghanaian colonel and wished to co-operate, but felt that they must lay down one condition.

'What is this condition?' asked Colonel Hansen.

'We demand only one thing in return for our co-operation', replied the chief. 'We have here the names of three

63

Baluba chiefs. They are wicked men and we want their heads.'

After a little more argument, the meeting broke up in confusion. A short time later I visited Tshiakiapa and had a meeting with the local administrators, the majority of whom were Lulua. On Hansen's advice I stressed the need for co-operation and tolerance between the tribes. This was agreed, and after a pleasant meeting we adjourned to the mess for a drink. At the mess the head administrator took Hansen aside and said that, in spite of this meeting, he still wished the Ghana contingent to co-operate in ejecting all the Baluba from Tshiakiapa. Hansen nearly had a stroke.

The position was further complicated by the rivalry between the chiefs and the young administrators who had been appointed by the provincial government. When the Belgian-organised administration broke down, the chiefs saw their chance of obtaining even more power than they had wielded previously. On the other hand, the young up-and-coming and politically minded administrators had very different intentions. As a result, these two groups, although belonging to the same tribe, were working in different directions.

In Luluaburg itself, the provincial government was loyal to the central government. But this did not make all plain sailing; many of the officials had a sentimental regard for the aims of Lumumba and regretted his fall from grace, and this led to grave suspicion between them and the local Congolese garrison. Brigadier Michel, the brigade commander, was always having to patch matters up. The biggest headache of all, however, was 'King' Kalonji himself. As he did not appear to have much difficulty in obtaining arms and equipment from outside, more and more of his untrained men were carrying modern weapons. With very few exceptions his army lacked any discipline. One battalion of the Ghana regiment went to Bakwakanga, the capital of Kalonji's territory. Kalonji classed Ghana as a communist country and so it is greatly to the credit of Colonel Thompson, a Green Jacket who commanded this battalion, that the friction between the Ghanaians and the Baluba was not more serious.

At first, when I visited Luluaburg, I avoided going to see 'King' Kalonji, partly because I did not wish to interfere in United Nations affairs (for the UN did not recognise Kalonji), and partly because I feared that President Nkrumah might suspect my motives in talking to this man. Brigadier Michel and Colonels Thompson and Ankrah together managed to keep him reasonably under control, but there came a time when I thought that a visit to him might serve some useful purpose. We therefore arranged a meeting through Colonel Thompson. His Belgian military adviser conducted us to the building in which the 'king' worked. Outside his office was a milling mass of soldiers, armed to the teeth, chiefs and hangers-on. Eventually we were conducted to the 'presence'.

Kalonji refused to shake hands, because, having been crowned 'king', he was too scared to shake hands with anybody. He dilated at length on the evils of the Lulua, and what he proposed to do about it, eventually producing a photostat map showing the territory he proposed to conquer. I studied this map with interest and then put it in my pocket—much to the annoyance of Kalonji. I later delivered it to General McKeown (the new Irish commander of the UN military forces) in Leopoldville. I told Kalonji that if he tried to make his soldiers go out of their tribal territory, this would be resisted by the Ghana troops and that if his troops became really troublesome it was probable that United Nations headquarters would send reinforcements to Kasai and deal with him properly. I also said that it would be wise for him to draw a lesson from the fate of Lumumba. I had warned Lumumba that if he encouraged his army to violence this army would eventually turn on him, and I forecast that the same would probably happen to Kalonji if he was not careful. As far as I know, Kalonji later had a spell in jail, but whether through the action of his unruly troops or not I do not know. Kalonji just laughed and produced samples of primitive weapons which he said could be manufactured in Bakwakanga. He further stated that if the United Nations did get difficult, and in particular if Indian troops came to his territory, the Kalonjists would fight. We did not take this very seriously; the Indians could have made mincemeat out of the Kalonjist rabble. Eventually, our interview ended and I came away feeling sorry for the Belgian military adviser, who had to work in this atmosphere and seemed a reasonable enough man.

The longer the Ghana army stayed in these territories the more friendly they became with the local inhabitants and the

65

Congolese garrisons. Being by nature a suspicious person, I never trusted the Congolese soldier, because no one could ever predict what he might do when full of drink and the 'weed'. On my tours round detachments I repeatedly told the troops not to forget that they were soldiers and never to let themselves get in a position where they could be overwhelmed by the Congolese, either tribesmen or troops. But the Ghanaian is by nature very friendly and much more trusting than was justifiable under such circumstances. This led to tragedies: at Port Franqui 120 Ghanaian soldiers with their British officers were murdered, and there was a similar horrible affair at a railway junction on the borders of Baluba and Lulua territory. To describe the incident at Port Franqui would open old wounds and is better left alone, but the other incident serves as an example of the treachery and primitive savagery with which all United Nations soldiers had to contend.

On the border between Lulua and Baluba territory there was a small railway station where the Lulua engine driver and his fireman left the train and a Baluba engine driver and fireman took over. A platoon of Ghanaians under a British national service officer was stationed here to supervise the change-over. Some three miles from the railway station the Kalonjists had a post occupied by about 250 men. One morning they arrived to arrest the Lulua engine driver and his fireman. This, of course, was resisted by the Ghanaian guard. Firing broke out. During the short engagement two Kalonjists were killed and a Kalonjist sergeant severely wounded. The Kalonjists then decided that they had had enough. They had no transport and asked to borrow the Ghanaians land rover to get their wounded back to camp. After some discussion the Ghanaian platoon sergeant volunteered to accompany the land rover's driver. Neither of them was ever seen again. They were undoubtedly murdered by the Kalonjists.

Many of the atrocities committed in the Congo have never received proper publicity, and it is only recently that crimes like the murder of priests in Northern Katanga have come to the public's notice. The murders in Port Franqui were a far greater crime than most. This murder was committed, not by roving tribesmen, but by Mobutu's soldiers. As far as I know the perpetrators have never been brought to justice.

66

2. *The Third Battalion Mutiny*

Life in the Congo was naturally very demoralising for the soldier, particularly for those troops who had not had any previous overseas service—that is, the vast majority. There was nothing conducive to maintaining morale and confidence in the higher leadership. Later in this book I deal in general with the requirements of a United Nations military force and do not wish to harp upon the ineffectiveness of the orders given to troops serving under United Nations command, because there are many explanations—some valid and some invalid—for this state of affairs. But I think, perhaps, that I might give one instance of the difficulties.

In August 1960, I had a passage of words with Dr Bunche, for whom I have the greatest respect, over the difficulties of soldiers working under the existing orders, and told the Ghana Brigade headquarters in Leopoldville to ask for clarification on certain aspects of such orders as there were. On August 21, the brigade major rang up a Major Berthiaume and asked for clarification of a paragraph in an order, which said: 'If a UN person is arrested, explain diplomatic immunity, etc.' A conversation on these lines ensued:

> Brigade Major: 'What action is to be taken if a person is threatened by a weapon?'
> Berthiaume consulted Dr Bunche, and said: 'The arrest must not be resisted; the UN person on the spot who has not been arrested must effect a strategic withdrawal and allow the arrest to continue.'
> Brigade Major: 'UN Operation Directive No 2, just received, states that "unless members of a UN force are clearly employed on some serious breach of law, every peaceful effort must be made to prevent the arrest or effect his release". Should this be interpreted on the lines of your answer to my previous question?'
> Berthiaume: 'Yes.'

This meant, in fact, that a UN officer, soldier or civilian could be arrested and beaten up by Congolese and no effective action could be taken by UN soldiers witnessing the event. From the

67

morale point of view, it was an impossible situation and the simple soldier found it very difficult to understand why things like this were allowed to take place. This was not the only drain on morale. In a place like Tshiakiapa, where the Third Battalion of the Ghana army mutinied, it was all work and no play, as was the case in many other parts of the Congo. The Congolese soldiers were poorly commanded and rampaged when they had had drink; beer was plentiful and Indian hemp, which grows in profusion in parts of the Congo, such as Tshiakiapa, is a great courage-booster. Many of the Congolese women did not appear to have very high morals. Therefore the soldier in his spare time was inclined to fall back on wine, women and hemp. We in the Ghana army tried to limit the length of tour of the battalions for this very reason. The lack of clear direction from United Nations headquarters in Leopoldville, the atmosphere of hate, and the language barrier alone would place a severe strain on even the most mature soldier. It certainly placed a very grave strain on the African soldier, very often led by inexperienced officers.

The Third Battalion of the Ghana army had done a first class job of work in Leopoldville prior to going to Tshiakiapa, and it came through the first trying times with flying colours. It was commanded by David Hansen, a young Ghanaian who is now head of the Ghana navy. He possessed all the right ideas but was, of course, inexperienced and sometimes perhaps not very moderate in applying discipline. I would rather attribute the reasons for the mutiny to the wine, women and Indian hemp than to any other reason, but undoubtedly things came to a head when the men heard the rumour that their wives were to be moved from Accra to another barracks in Tamale (Northern Ghana), while they were still in the Congo. They also heard the rumour that some of their furniture was to be auctioned before the move, because it could not be fitted into the quarters at Tamale. These rumours as they reached the soldiers were either exaggerated or untrue, but they had a disastrous effect on a battalion which had already gone through a very trying time. The first I knew of any trouble was a signal one morning from Brigadier Michel, commanding the Ghana Brigade in the Congo, saying that serious trouble had occurred in the Third Battalion and that Hansen had been severely injured. Nkrumah was in his country house five or six miles from Accra, and I went to see him there. He took the news well, but agreed that I should proceed to Tshiakiapa at once to deal with the situation.

Away I went. On arrival at Luluaburg I was met by Joe Michel, who told me the gist of the story. He had flown down to Tshiakiapa with an old 'Gold Coaster', Major Duggie Cairns, the morning before. On arrival at Tshiakiapa airport he had found the majority of the battalion sitting on the ground, insisting on talking to the brigadier. A great many of them were full of liquor or drugs. After some hour or so of argument, he had persuaded the men to return to their billets and spent the rest of the day trying to find out what had happened. In brief, it transpired that Hansen had explained to all the non-commissioned officers that the wives of all the men would probably be moved to Tamale before the battalion returned to Ghana. The NCOs had not liked this, and had made it clear that the troops would not like it either. However, neither Hansen nor his second-in-command, Major Burns, anticipated any serious trouble. Hansen was in the mess at about seven o'clock the same evening when a Ghanaian officer came to him and said that the troops stationed on the airfield had marched back to release the prisoners and were in a state of mutiny outside the garrison, firing their rifles into the air. Hansen got his jeep and drove up the road. It was by then dark and difficult to see what was happening. Hansen managed to pacify the men for a moment, and then went into the orderly room where he was joined by other officers, including his British second-in-command. The crowd of soldiers gradually became angrier and noisier, so Hansen went out again to reason with them. He was heavily attacked with rifle butts and left for dead on the ground. The mob, about 200, ran riot. There is no doubt that the majority of them were full of liquor and hemp. They attacked the orderly room, from which the British and Ghanaian officers fled, attacked the quartermaster's stores, stealing all the ammunition, and broke into the officers' mess, stealing the drink. What well nigh amounted to a reign of terror lasted through the night, with the majority of the officers hiding in the bush. Burns, the second-in-command, and others managed to get Hansen into the medical orderly's room, where they found he was still alive. As dawn broke, Burns managed to persuade the men to go up to the airfield and await the arrival of the brigadier, to whom the officers had managed to send

69

a message on the one set which the mutineers had not broken.

After his visit, Michel had left Duggie Cairns at Tshiakiapa. Old Duggie is a very calm, experienced officer, and when we arrived at Tshiakiapa he was there to meet me with, to my astonishment, a guard of honour—a rather sulky guard of honour, but nevertheless quite a clean one. I said to Duggie: 'Shall I speak to the men here?' since many of them were lurking about the airport.

'No. I have arranged for you to speak to them in small parties at their billets. They are still in a dangerous mood.'

We spent the hours of the day touring the various detachments and I could but tell the men the seriousness of their actions, and warn them that if they did any more mutinous acts they would certainly suffer severe punishment when they returned to Ghana. There had been a good deal of firing during the previous night, but it was Duggie Cairns' view that this had been largely to get rid of some of the ammunition the men had acquired illegally; I told them to hand in the ammunition, that I would stay in Tshiakiapa for the night and that if there was any more firing I would not be responsible for the consequences!

In the meantime it was important to get the ring leaders back to Ghana as quickly as possible, to prevent any further trouble. We had to do this without their knowing that they were going to be arrested and put in jail once they got home. With the help of the officers we made a list of those we knew to be the ring leaders, of the doubtfuls who were to be isolated when they got back to Ghana, and of those who were completely innocent and should suffer no punishment. The British government, which had repeatedly come to the rescue of the Ghanaian contingent so far as aircraft were concerned, quickly responded to a request for a Britannia to start flying out this battalion, and when I left I was able to take back with me to Ghana the ninety known most dangerous men.

The punishment meted out to the men was severe, though many of the sentences I believe have since been either relaxed or annulled. Whatever the rights or wrongs of the soldiers' grievances, one could not accept this type of action in a young army.

Very few of the contingents serving in United Nations in the Congo have been without their troubles, and you cannot wholly blame the contingents. The main blame must rest upon the United Nations' military command who singularly failed to give any proper direction to the commanders, very seldom visited the detachments and in fact gave little guidance to the young, inexperienced leaders carrying out one of the most difficult operations which any soldier could conceive. The atmosphere of mutiny, murder and rape in which these soldiers had to live did nothing to help.

3. *Stanleyville Troops 'Attack' Luluaburg*

Later I was again sitting in my office in Accra when I received a cryptic message from Colonel Ankrah who, in the absence of Brigadier Michel, was commanding the Ghana contingent in Kasai province. It read somewhat like this: 'Stanleyville troops (Lumumbists) arriving Luluaburg. Suggest you visit.'

I had already read in various situation reports, and seen accounts in the popular press, of this impending collision between the Mobutu garrison at Luluaburg and the Stanleyville 'invaders'. It has always been my experience that the size of the threat under such circumstances is in inverse ratio to the size of the arrow on the map produced with the newspaper report describing the military situation. In any case very few reporters dared to leave Leopoldville at this time for fear of missing 'hot' news, and I therefore doubted whether they were aware of the true situation. All kinds of rumours of what in fact happened have since been given; a true description is enlightening. I sent a message to Colonel Ankrah saying that I was on my way, and would he please keep the airport clear. Quite naturally, the UN secretariat at New York was sensitive about visitors such as myself and I had always had to clear visits with New York. In this case it had to be done in rather a hurry!

On arrival at Luluaburg I was met at the airport by Colonel Ankrah who described to me the events to date. On hearing that the Stanleyville troops were on their way, the local garrison comander had immediately sought UN protection and had been evacuated to Leopoldville, together with several of his other 'gallant officers'. There were three Congolese battalions stationed in Luluaburg at the time; one appeared to want to join up with the Stanleyville troops, the other two wished to remain loyal to Mobutu, but did not want to fight. As the

71

Stanleyville troops arrived in the outskirts, Mobutu's soldiers had retreated to their barracks, thus giving the new arrivals a chance to rampage through the town, killing and beating up. Colonel Ankrah had eventually succeeded in ejecting them and had called a conference of officers from both sides. These officers were waiting at the local UN headquarters to see me. When I arrived they rapidly agreed that it was stupid to fight, that Mobutu's soldiers should put their weapons away in their barracks and the Stanleyville soldiers stack theirs at their existing camp site outside Stanleyville. The Stanleyville soldiers were a little annoyed because Colonel Ankrah had ejected them from the airport, but I was pleased since they had some anti-aircraft equipment. However, this was only a minor irritant at the conference.

Over a glass of beer, we agreed that at half past three in the afternoon Michel, who had now returned, Ankrah and I would visit both sides to make sure the terms of the agreement had been complied with, and the following day we would try to seek some solution to the impasse. The local inhabitants were antagonistic to the local garrison because of the atrocities it had committed in the past. After a good lunch we set off to find out how things were going. We got no further than the local barracks. When we arrived there we discovered a milling mass of excited soldiery. On such occasions we made it a point not to appear in force, for fear of frightening the Congolese into opening fire or taking some other stupid action. However, as a rule we did have a platoon or so within easy call. I have read of Major Lawson's courageous activities when he went about unarmed. When in small parties we always did the same, because even if you had a weapon you were so severely outnumbered that the weapon was not much use to you. What is more, the Congolese seemed to trust you much more if you did not carry a weapon. If you did, there was always the danger that they would assault you in order to take your revolver or whatever it might be.

It took us some time to discover the reason for the excitement in the barracks. Every now and then a jeep would drive up, loaded with savage-looking gendarmerie, bringing some blood-stained soldier or civilian, who was immediately pushed into the prison. These unfortunates turned out to be either

Stanleyville soldiers or members of the provincial cabinet. What had happened was this: when the officers arrived back at the barracks after their conference, the soldiers, outraged at being told to put their weapons away, arrested all their officers and put them in jail. They also sent patrols throughout the town to arrest the cabinet, because they thought that the Stanleyville 'attack' had been arranged by them.

So there we were, faced by two thousand or so soldiers with no officers, and with the cabinet in the lock-up. There was little chance of doing anything about the Stanleyville troops that day; our only course was to try to get the officers and the cabinet released. Michel and I said that we did not propose to leave the barracks until they released the prisoners, but the excited soldiery showed few signs of co-operating. We stayed outside the jail asking and pleading until, at about seven o'clock, we came to a compromise. The self-appointed leaders agreed to release all the cabinet and to discuss the position of the officers the following day. Slowly, bedraggled cabinet ministers trooped out from the jail. It was just getting dark. We thought it best to have them clear of the barracks before there was a change of mind. The only transport available was a land rover belonging to the Ghana contingent and the car in which we had arrived. These were stuffed with the ex-prisoners and then despatched smartly into the blue. Joe Michel and I found ourselves left out of the party, and we spent a somewhat uneasy three-quarters of an hour waiting for the transport to return. Two of the cabinet ministers had also been left behind, but we hid them in a clump of bushes for fear that some soldier might take a dislike to them. Our transport eventually returned and we sped to Michel's house for a strong drink.

The next day we had the problem of what we could do for the arrested officers, and of finding out what had happened to the Stanleyville group. No one could find the latter, so we sent a light aircraft to search. The pilot found a small column of trucks hurrying north. The Stanleyville 'attackers', who I think numbered more like 200 than the 2,000 described in the press, had evidently decided they had had enough. I suspect they had been misled into thinking that the Ghanaian troops would join them in dealing with Mobutu's men.

On the previous day we had placed road blocks at the exits

to the barracks to prevent Mobutu's soldiers coming out armed. That morning, at the main road block, we had a long conversation with the gendarmerie (the fierce boys).

One of them approached me rather sadly and said: 'What are we to do, General? We have thrown out all our Belgian officers and appointed others. These others have now all become politicians and we have arrested them. We now have no officers. What are we to do?'

I scratched my head, and I could only reply: 'I suppose you had better elect another lot.'

Such was the condition. Parleying with the Congolese is a most exhausting business, as anyone who has served in the Congo will agree, and it was impossible to obtain the release of the so-called officers before my return to Ghana. Subsequently, Joe Michel obtained agreement that those in jail would be released provided we lifted the road blocks. The road blocks were lifted, the officers released and Mobutu's soldiers rampaged through the African quarter, killing about forty civilians. Such was the daily round of the soldier serving the UN, and such was the value of 'negotiation' in such circumstances.

7 Military Problems

1. *Africanisation*

MUCH discussion has taken place on how the problem of the Congolese army should or should not have been tackled, and of course many people disagreed with my original conviction that you would never produce true peace in the Congo unless the Congolese army was reformed and retrained. In preceding chapters I have tried to illustrate the unreliability of the many factions which reared their heads in this army, but some basic facts still remain to be highlighted. The *Force Publique* was organised by the Belgians, largely on the tribal system, units being stationed outside their tribal area and used to stop tribal warfare and maintain law and order. As long as European officers led these troops, some degree of restraint could be imposed upon them. By African standards it was a large army—some 25,000 men—well equipped and well accommodated. The Belgians had made the mistake, so common among ex-colonial powers, of delaying the training of Congolese officers; when the white officers were ejected the Congolese army was lost. They could not even feed themselves, let alone impose discipline.

It is too late now to do what I would have liked to have seen done at the beginning. In brief, what I suggested to the United Nations secretariat was that the United Nations should organise an extensive training scheme for the Congolese army, including the army of Katanga. This would have given them something to do other than running riot, murdering and plundering, and gradually a reliable army might have been built up.

However, nothing came of my suggestion. Generals take time to train, and even the most well-intentioned Congolese who becomes one in a period of months cannot hope to lead an army the size of the ANC. Had the United Nations not had difficulties with this army, the job of stopping tribal warfare would have been reasonably simple.

I had no real experience of the Katangan army, but I have talked to those who have and I have no reason to doubt that, by and large, this army was better disciplined than any other section of the armed forces in the Congo. Even so, it would surely not have been difficult to include the Katangan army in the overall retraining scheme instead of trying to treat it as a separate entity. Unless the Katangans had been included, it would have been politically impossible to put through a retraining scheme for the others. It has also been argued that the Katangan army was so much better than those loyal either to Mobutu or to Lumumba because of the 'mercenaries' employed. This argument has an element of truth in it, since many of the mercenaries were dedicated, efficient soldiers. Others, of course, were not, but were mere adventurers out for personal gain. Unfortunately, in this difficult situation the West, UN, or anybody else could not have life both ways. You cannot, for example, oppose and deplore the supply of arms and equipment to a secessionist movement based on Stanleyville, and at the same time condone the supply of similar armaments and equipment to Tshombe and 'King' Kalonji. I have met Stanleyville soldiers, Kalonjist and Mobutu soldiers: none seemed any better or any worse than the other. They all longed for help and retraining. It would, perhaps, have been possible to include some of the better mercenaries in a United Nations retraining mission.

The precipitate removal of the Belgian officers from the ANC and later that of myself and my fellow British officers from the Ghana armed forces highlighted a trend which has recently been followed in Tanzania, Uganda and Kenya. Since my departure a British military mission has been established in Ghana. Their loyalty is to the United Kingdom High Commissioner and they advise the Ghanaian officers who hold executive positions in the armed forces, from the highest to the lowest. When I returned from Ghana, I warned the authorities that this action in Ghana was not exceptional, but, I thought, typical of a trend liable to be followed in other African territories, particularly in East Africa.

Africanisation of the Ghana army had been carried out more rapidly than in any other ex-colonial army, but yet it was not quick enough. There were several reasons for this, not just one. The African officers see their fellow countrymen, many of lower educational qualification and less experience, becoming highly ranked politicians and highly paid civil servants. Their progress by comparison seems very slow and this breeds envy and jealousy. The education of Sandhurst and similar service institutions leads the young man to consider himself a cut above most of his fellow Africans. He sees every other department of national life being Africanised rapidly, while the armed forces seem to lag. It is natural that he becomes impatient and covets the appointment of, say, his British commanding officer. The less balanced of the African officers therefore become easy prey to left wing, communist and nationalist propaganda. The solution to this problem is simple; it is to establish military missions on the lines of those existing already in Ghana and other countries. Nevertheless, I am afraid that there may be further instances in Africa of armies seizing power, and probably further instances of British officers undergoing unpleasant experiences.

In young countries the maxim 'might is right' makes sense. Infiltration of the armed forces is a most obvious and productive aim for communists. If the leaders of these armed forces are pro-communist and succeed in overthrowing the existing government, the East has had a success. African leaders, President Nkrumah included, would be well advised to keep the size of their armed forces down to the level which allows them to be officered by experienced reliable men. This is a slow business and for prestige reasons some African leaders will find it a hard rule to adhere to, although it is in their interest to do so.

Another way of guarding against military coups is to keep a balance between the size of the army, police, navy and air force, if the latter two exist. This technique has been used successfully in some South American countries where leaders have sometimes been saved by one or another of the armed forces remaining loyal. Perhaps we would have been saved a lot of trouble in East Africa if we had read the lessons of the Congo and Ghana more intelligently.

The instinct and training of the British officer makes him rebel against brigadiers' being created after three years' service, and the fall off of efficiency resulting from the withdrawal of the British officers hurts. But reality has to be faced and if we do not withdraw our officers and NCOs gracefully into military missions while the going is still good, further unpleasant things will happen.

2. *UN's difficulties, limitations and achievements*

The United Nations' efforts in the Congo have been continually under attack, either from the West or from the East. Possibly this shows that they have done a good, neutral job of work. What, in fact, has been achieved? There is no doubt that the United Nations could have done better in the Congo, but I think it is safe to say that the blame for not having done so does not rest entirely with its personnel. In tackling a task so immense as trying to restore peace, tranquillity and good government to the Congo, it was wholly inadequately equipped. Had the job been entrusted to some major power, such as the United States, the United Kingdom or Russia, each undoubtedly could have done a better job in its different way. The United Nations had nothing to work on. It had no clear idea of the problem when it arrived. There was no staff organised to cope with the total breakdown in a country of this size, without any administration, law and order non-existent and hardly any trained Congolese personnel to build upon. Maybe the countries of Africa have to be granted independence before they are ready for it, and maybe the world has to suffer chaos in parts of Africa for many years to come. This does not mean that the heroic efforts made by many individuals working for the United Nations in the Congo should be disparaged. Individuals such as Brian Urquhart, Ivan Smith, Robert Gardiner and General Rikhye are not the fools that many people think. They are gallant and dedicated men who have done what they think is right, irrespective of whether London, Washington or Moscow agrees—and, besides, it is most unlikely that these would all agree at the same time!

At one time the Ghana Brigade had a battalion stationed

at an old Belgian pleasure resort, Lac Makamba. This was a territory owned by a tribe called the Luntu, over which Kalonji cast covetous eyes. The Ghanaian soldiers prevented Kalonji from invading the area. When the Ghana battalion was withdrawn and could not be replaced, due to shortage of UN troops, Kalonji attacked, killing 400 Luntu. The Luntu were armed with bows and arrows, the Kalonjists with Belgian and Italian weapons.

Thousands of lives have been saved by United Nations troops. Thousands of lives have been saved by United Nations Food Relief and Medical Assistance. There is absolutely no doubt that had the United Nations been forced to withdraw earlier from the Congo, due to lack of soldiers and lack of support from member nations, the Soviet bloc, the Chinese and the Casablanca group of countries would have given overt assistance to the Stanleyville regime, and I assume that conversely the West would have been forced to give overt assistance elsewhere. This is the trend now that the UN has withdrawn.

President Nkrumah was quite honest when he said that he wished to keep the cold war out of the Congo. The Americans, the British, the Belgians and many others also wished to keep the cold war out of the Congo, but, of course, their wish was conditional on the ultimate solutions being favourable to themselves. The UN has at least been trying to produce a solution favourable to the Congolese, and has done more to this end than any embassy official of any power, great or small. It is sad to think that many Western diplomatists have regarded the UN headquarters as working against the interests of the West, because this was not in fact the case.

In spite of the money and effort which the United Nations has poured into the Congo, peace has not returned. Outbreaks of lawlessness continue to erupt. No-one is safe. The basic reasons for this are now obvious to everybody. The United Nations military forces went into the Congo to 'assist' the central government in Leopoldville to maintain law and order, but unfortunately the major law-breakers were the Congolese army—the ANC. Had the United Nations forces been allowed to discipline and retrain this force, probably disbanding a portion of it, things might have been different. Had the orders to the United Nations troops been framed by somebody with military experience and not written as political documents, things might have been different. The United Nations forces have now left the Congo. I fear that it will be a long time before the ex-Belgian Congo will rebuild itself in peace. It is moreover, now wide open to Chinese and Russian penetration.

The Belgian policy of paternalism did not help. Practically no Congolese were trained as administrators, as military commanders or in any of the professions. For example, prior to independence there were only twelve Congolese who had ever been to a university. The sudden withdrawal of Belgians from the Congo left a vacuum which could not be filled. The result was chaos, and this chaos must have been felt outside the Congo. For example, the soldiers of Uganda saw with their own eyes how soldiers in the Congolese army behaved. Conditions in the Congo may not have contributed to the mutinies in Kenya, Tanganyika and Uganda, but on the other hand they may well have done so.

The African leaders in these countries have at least learnt one lesson from the Congo; you cannot establish a political solution or political stability if mutinous soldiery is allowed to function unrestrained. I can remember the late Dag Hammarskjold telling me that it was a political, not a military problem in the Congo. How wrong he was.

Most of what I have said so far in Part Two of this book are either stories or extracts from happenings in the Congo none of which probably leads anywhere in trying to answer the bigger problem of what could have been and can be done to bring peace and prosperity back to the country. The problem is, and all along has been, such a difficult one that it is hard to draw any satisfactory conclusions from the maze of contradictions which have gone to make up the 'Congo dilemma'. Nevertheless, it is important for the future of Africa and of the Congo itself to try to draw some lessons from what has happened.

As I have already hinted, it always seemed to me that right from the beginning neither the West nor the East was interested primarily in producing a solution satisfactory to the Congolese people as a whole; each bloc pursued its own interest. It may be argued that this was because neither side understood the basic facts of the Congo crisis; but this, I think, is questionable since all countries had qualified ambassadorial representatives in

Leopoldville who must have realised the difficulties facing the United Nations. There were individuals inside United Nations headquarters both in Leopoldville and New York who fully understood the problem and I am sure that on many occasions these people tried to explain them to the diplomatists. Admittedly, due to the wish to maintain the correct 'neutralist' appearance at United Nations headquarters, the machinery for producing results was in many cases inefficient, but it could have been much more efficient had outside criticism been more constructive.

It is easy to be wise after the event, but certain basic truths which I defy anyone to deny have emerged sooner or later during this sad story. Basically it is true that when the Belgians handed over power to the Congolese there was not a single Congolese fit to hold high office in the central government set up to run the independent Congo. This, of course, meant that they needed the assistance of outside administrators. At the beginning, the Belgians themselves—most suitable for the task from the point of view of language and experience—were not acceptable politically, nor were representatives of the ex-colonial and Eastern powers, because their judgements and advice were always suspected of being clouded by the particular interest of the country or power bloc of their origin. For this very reason, the only machinery which could provide assistance to the new Congo without intensifying the cold war struggle was that of the United Nations. I do not think that anyone will now deny that had the nettle of controlling the Congolese army been grasped earlier, much waste of life and money would have been avoided and stability obtained far more quickly. It was a situation in which neither the East nor the West could expect to win outright. Almost overnight the country, outwardly civilised at least in the main cities, illustrated how thin this veneer of civilisation was. It will be many years before the situation throughout the Congo is restored, even to the extent of the country's getting back to the position it was in just prior to independence.

I think the Russians realised more quickly than the West that they gained nothing by trying to compete with the chaos and unreliability of the Congolese politician, and therefore they were content that chaos should continue. After all, they did not need to win—all they needed to do was to help create a situation in which the West was denied the economic advantages which a stable Congo could give. In many ways the West seems to have been much less subtle and much too positive in its approach to the problem. Anything the United Nations did which might seem to be even neutralist, as opposed to pro-Western, was labelled as anti-Western. The United Kingdom came strongly out on the side of General Mobutu, largely, I think, because he was against Lumumba and had ejected the Russian embassy from Leopoldville. The fact that hardly any soldiers in the army would obey his orders was, it seems, immaterial. A strong, unified Congo under a powerful central government is a pipe-dream, whatever paper arguments may be made for it, for neither the administrative knowledge nor the ability yet exists among the Congolese to bring this about. Moreover, tribal allegiances are still so strong that loyalty to the tribe will, for a long time, take priority over any loyalty to a distant, mythical central government sitting in Leopoldville.

It seems to me that the West has always been too frightened of the extent to which Leopoldville could physically control the affairs of Katanga. As a 'neutralist' I met most of the high United Nations officials serving in the Congo during the first year, and apart from one or two—such as a general from Guinea who was not really on the staff of the United Nations headquarters at all—I cannot name one who was working either for or against the communists as such. Their whole aim seemed to be to produce a solution which would help the Congolese people, whether or not the solution was entirely acceptable to East or West. Although President Nkrumah often said, and tried to do, some things which were poison to the West, I do not believe that his conduct was any worse than that of certain Western diplomatists. The trouble was that he shouted about it too much and therefore received a great deal of publicity.

What the United Nations has needed throughout is effective support and the services of good, experienced men who could help to produce solutions to the many problems facing the Congo. Although at the start it was politically impossible for members of the larger nations to have people in high positions, many of the more junior posts could have been occupied by experienced nationals from these countries.

What did horrify me when I finally returned to Britain was

the apparent lack of knowledge of the true situation in the Congo. It is inadvisable to name any particular individuals, but I give five examples.

1 One evening in London I met some members of parliament who were interested in Katanga. In conversation with one of them I asked him why, in fact, he was a member of a Katanga 'lobby'. He replied that really he knew nothing about the Congo, but that all his friends were members of the 'lobby' and therefore he had joined.

2 On another occasion I was asked by an official in the Foreign Office for my views on what was currently happening in the Congo. I gave them, and received the amazing comment: 'I am glad you see some hope, General, because really this problem is a hell of a bore.'

3 I talked to a member of parliament who had spent two days in Leopoldville; this was the full extent of his Congo experience. Yet now he poses as an expert.

4 Not so very long ago I was listening to an early morning broadcast where two members of parliament were discussing the fact that the United Nations had now withdrawn from the Congo. The comment of one of them was interesting: 'Jolly good show; they only added to the chaos.'

5 Lastly, a story I heard the other day which I think is true. During some of the time Robert Gardiner, the well known Ghanaian United Nations official, was the secretary-general's representative in the Congo. One evening the British ambassador got him on the telephone and was very agitated. The conversation went something like this: 'Look here, Robert, a lot of Congolese students are round the embassy making a hell of a racket and threatening to break the place down. Can't you people do anything to protect me?' Robert Gardiner, who knew many of the students, hurried round to the embassy. From the wall surrounding it, he addressed the crowd and persuaded them to go home. He then went into the embassy itself to see the ambassador. The ambassador was all over him. 'Thank you very much, Robert. Marvellous! You must need a drink after that.' Robert's reply was, 'I would love one, but don't let me interfere with your report to Lord Home that the United Nations are still creating chaos in the Congo.'

3. *Problems of a United Nations Military Task Force*

I do not know whether a United Nations military command will ever become a fact, but I still hope that, with Western backing, one will be created. However, I hold the view that for various reasons the dispatch of United Nations forces to a country under circumstances similar to those in the ex-Belgian Congo was a great waste of money. It would be well therefore to review the military lessons which can be drawn from this sad affair.

United Nations' military intervention is being suggested, more and more frequently, as a means of preventing a clash between the major powers or, under certain circumstances, as a substitute for the re-entry of an ex-colonial power into a newly independent territory.

I have some strong feelings on the weaknesses displayed in the military conduct of recent operations in the Congo. Many will say that to rectify the defects I criticise is impossible, since the political difficulties encountered at United Nations headquarters in New York rule out any agreement on such matters. That is as may be; but it seems pointless for countries like the United Kingdom to pour money into the United Nations efforts if, because of the ineffectiveness of the military command, largely due to restrictions placed on them by orders from New York, these efforts are bound to fail.

It is a principal requisite of any military operation that the commander, when he is appointed, should receive a clear directive. Yet, at the start of operations in the Congo, no soldier, from the commander downwards, had a clear idea of why he was there or what he was supposed to achieve. I am sure it was thought that the mere presence of blue helmeted 'Peace Soldiers' would restore peace and tranquillity to the Congo. When dealing with an emotional, excited people, many of whom are not very civilised, there is faint hope of such expectations being realised.

From the start, the commanders of both civil and military operations in the Congo suffered from excessive control by New York. Scarcely any move could be made without a telephone call to the United Nations secretariat, though conditions in the Congo changed hourly. Provided always that the commanders appointed are of sufficient calibre, more trust must be placed in them to do the right thing at the right time. There is great need for the commanders who are appointed to control United Nations military operations in any particular part of the world to have understanding of the peoples and conditions with which he will have to deal. A soldier with knowledge only of Europe and European peoples can be quite at sea when dealing with African soldiers, whose actions, by European standards, are sometimes quite unpredictable.

The various vicissitudes and setbacks encountered in the military effort during the Congo operations are by now old news, and I do not wish to linger over them. However, it might be of interest if I catalogued some of the lessons which we who served in the Ghana armed forces drew from this trying Congo affair. These are:

1. *We believe that if similar operations are to be carried out by United Nations in the future, a military planning cell is required at United Nations headquarters in New York, possessing knowledge of the military resources which might, in certain eventualities, be placed at the disposal of the United Nations by member countries.*

This cell should have a proper intelligence system with knowledge of the conditions in the country in question, particularly the armaments and the attitude of the local armed forces, and have in mind a suitable command and staff organisation to handle United Nations operations.

The fly-in of the first contingents to Leopoldville and other places was a nightmare for the few officers who happened to be in the Congo at the time. There was no appointed military commander, there was no plan about what to do with the contingents when they arrived, and there were no communications. They just arrived, and those who came to Leopoldville were deployed by the Ghana Brigade headquarters on an *ad hoc* unauthorised basis.

2. *The contingents which are flown in must be properly equipped to cope with the role envisaged.*

I doubt if anyone at United Nations headquarters had any idea what the troops were supposed to do when they

85

arrived in the Congo. Only if there is a properly organised military planning cell and intelligence system at the UN can such shortcomings be overcome in the future.

3. *Soldiers are taught to fight. They are also taught to function on clear orders. It is absolutely essential that contingent commanders, and the troops under their command, have clear-cut orders, if disasters and nonsenses are not to occur.*

Some civilians seem to think that, in a situation of chaos such as has existed in the Congo, all will be well provided that you produce a satisfactory political situation. We in Ghana, particularly the officers in the armed forces, have always maintained that where a chaotic military situation exists you cannot produce a satisfactory political solution until you have stabilised the military situation. That it has taken so long to produce any semblance of order in the Congo is largely because this misconception has so long persisted. It must not be forgotten that the leaders of mutinous soldiers very often have their own political ambitions, and find argument with unarmed politicians far more fruitful if they go to the conference table carrying a gun.

4. *If member countries of the United Nations are found willing to contribute to the United Nations military effort, they should have a part of their military force organised so that it can be administratively self-supporting.*

In Africa, this would have to include a small air force group equipped with such types of aeroplanes as the Beaver and Otter, because ground communications in this continent are so poor. The United Nations had no idea how it was going to support the various contingents which were flown into the Congo in such great haste.

5. *Troops committed to serve in conditions similar to those which existed in the Congo should not be kept there for too long.*

The conduct of mutinous soldiers, the drink, the Indian hemp and the atmosphere of murder and disorder were not good for the young armies of Africa. These conditions, coupled with doubt as to the purpose of their being there, the lack of clear orders and the inability to make appropriate use of force to put things right when necessary, all contributed to undermine the morale and the reliability of the soldiers. I do not believe that there is a single contingent which has not had trouble with its troops, either in the Congo itself or when they have returned to their parent country.

There are enough lessons to be drawn from the Congo operation to fill a book, but I think I have referred to most of the important military ones. A commander confronted with the task of controlling a United Nations army drawn from many nations has one of the most difficult tasks which any soldier can be asked to perform. Every contingent differs in efficiency, in training and equipment, in temperament and sometimes in the political outlook of its soldiers. On top of this, a commander himself may have to be drawn from a so-called 'neutral' country. Neutral countries do not always produce experienced commanders, and for this reason alone it is essential that at least some of the points I have stressed are cleared up before the United Nations is again called upon to indulge in military exercises.

No doubt solutions to the many political problems facing the United Nations are bound always to be a matter of unhappy compromise. But where soldiers are to be deployed and asked to risk their lives in assisting to produce solutions, let us try to avoid the military mistakes of the disastrously expensive Congo crisis.

III

DISMISSAL, ANECDOTES, AND REFLECTIONS

8　Sacked by Nkrumah

WHEN, early in 1960, I heard that President Nkrumah was to pay a long visit to countries behind the Iron Curtain, I was naturally filled with a certain apprehension. I knew that the Russians had written a paper criticising the British training of Ghana's armed forces and I felt quite certain that they would leave no stone unturned to disrupt this training scheme. I had already set up a board to study the speeding-up of Africanisation in Ghana's armed forces, and Nkrumah himself seemed reasonably satisfied with progress in this direction—although it was clear that he was under pressure, even from within the country, to get rid of British officers, regardless of the effect on the expansion and efficiency of the units. I had various indications during Nkrumah's absence of the continuance of such pressure. It culminated in an order I received to send 400 potential officers to Moscow for military training. These were to depart within a fortnight from my receiving the order. I pointed out to the then minister of Defence, Mr de Graft Dickson, that, not counting the dangers the President faced by splitting the training of his army in two, it would be quite impossible within the time limit to produce the required number of young men sufficiently well educated. In any case, the time factor made the execution of the President's orders quite impossible, even if suitable material had existed. I also sent a message to Nkrumah himself, imploring him to reconsider his decision.

Mr de Graft Dickson's reply was that we should include in

the party some of the potential specialists rejected for service with the air force. This suggestion was completely fantastic, because these men lacked basic education and had even been rejected for 'other rank' ground staff work in the air force. For Ghana's Academy we set a minimum standard of education; the boys had to pass a written examination and an interview. At that time the country was producing just under 700 boys each year who were up to that standard, but many of these were required outside the armed services. 120 young men had just been selected to go to the Ghana Military Academy; if to these had been added 400 to go to Russia, there would have been precious few left for the many other essential jobs outside the armed services. Nevertheless, de Graft Dickson told me to get on with it, although I explained that it was an impossibility. I had to tell him I could not accept responsibility for executing an order which was impossible; nor could I accept responsibility for lowering the standard required without first discussing this with the President as Commander-in-Chief.

I feel quite sure now that a good deal of political capital was made against me over this question, but I do not think that any commander could accept orders undermining, firstly, the standard of the officer corps and, secondly, the long-term security of the country. Whether these young men come back to Ghana as budding communists or not is not the point. They will certainly not come back like-minded to the present officer corps. This must represent a long-term threat to Nkrumah's own position. I made it quite clear to Mr de Graft Dickson and also to the cabinet that I could not accept the responsibility for this state of affairs. I had had so many things to try me already and felt that now I must make a stand. In fact I was in the 'hole' which Colonel Coates (the us military attaché) had predicted. I was censured for communicating with the President direct and not through the Presidential Commission. But my argument was that the President, as my Commander-in-Chief, had taken a major policy decision without discussing it with me, and in any case, unless he was prepared to hear and listen to my arguments my position became impossible. It could be argued that circumstances similar to this had occurred before and that I had not made an issue of them. That may be true, but in previous cases we usually found a way out. As the President was still away and

the order had to be complied with in his absence there was no
way out. Either I had to make a stand and risk resignation or
the sack, or submit to an order which my military experience
told me would be quite wrong.

In the event, of course, President Nkrumah dismissed me
and I expect that this issue was one of the nails in my coffin—
but not all the nails. He had obviously been under pressure from
various people to get rid of me for political reasons. It could
justly be argued that the presence of a white 'imperialist' general
at the head of his armed forces prejudiced his own position as
the champion of anti-colonialism. I am sure that this latter argument was the one which carried most weight. It is, of course,
true that the method by which he dismissed me and other officers
was not exactly polite; at the time I was deeply hurt.

Nkrumah went about it in this way. Usually I saw him
about three times a week, but when he returned from Russia he
failed to send for me. As I had a number of matters which I had
to see him about, notably the dispatch of potential officers to
Russia for training, I sent him a note asking for an early interview. I received no reply. On the afternoon of the tenth day after
his return I received a message that he wished to see me at seven
o'clock in the evening accompanied by the then Brigadier Otu.
On arrival at Flagstaff House I was asked to wait, and after
waiting for half an hour or so, Geoffrey Bing came out of the
President's office and told me that Nkrumah was now ready to
see me, with Otu. Otu and I entered. Nkrumah was standing
behind his desk and was obviously in a very excited state. He
handed me a note, a copy of which is at Appendix F of this book;
I read it and said nothing. Nkrumah then started speaking. He
said he was grateful for all the assistance I had given him but
that in view of the British government's attitude throughout
Africa he wished me to hand over my job as Chief of Defence
Staff at once and that, in addition, all British officers were
relieved of their posts. I replied that I appreciated his anxiety to
Africanise his armed forces, but that if he went about it this way
not only would it upset the continuity of the training and expansion of these armed forces, but also politically it could not do
him very much good, particularly coming just before the
Queen's projected visit to Ghana. He said that the political
advantages of getting rid of the British officers far outweighed

93

any other considerations and that he really did not mind if his army was reduced to one battalion if in doing so it was possible to remove the British officers.

I saw that Nkrumah had worked himself into a state and it was very little use arguing with him. I said that if this was what he wanted of course it must be carried through, but when did he wish me to hand over to Otu and when did he wish British officers to be relieved of their posts? He replied: 'Immediately. You will hand over to Otu now and the British officers will hand over their posts tomorrow.' It would all be announced on Radio Ghana at nine that evening and therefore, even if he had wanted to, he could not now stop the rate of the change. This was typical. Having steeled himself to do something which he did not really like doing, he wished to get it over and done with. There was no point in arguing, so I said goodnight and left the office with Otu.

I was naturally very upset, but there was one amusing side-light to the proceedings. As we walked down the passage away from the President's office, Otu turned to me and said: 'General, excuse me for bothering you at this time, but can you possibly lend me some Major-General's insignia?'

I was also terribly disappointed that much of the work that so many British officers and senior Ghanaians had put into building up efficient armed forces should be thrown overboard, overnight.

But now I better understand why Nkrumah acted in the way he did. 'Seek ye first the political kingdom', he has said. This is what he was doing. He knew perfectly well that many of his dreams for the most efficient armed forces in Africa were being cast aside, but he was prepared to pay this price in his search for the 'political kingdom'. I like to think that he had at that time no personal animosity towards me; I had at least tried to advise him honestly. Since then, certain newspaper articles may have built up such animosity; if this is the case I am profoundly sorry, because I still have a great affection for him.

As soon as Nkrumah had arrived back from the East, I had forwarded to him the preliminary recommendations of the Ghanaianisation Board. It stated that the army could be fully Ghanaianised by January 1, 1963, on which date the British officers required to stay could be transferred to a military

94

mission. Had the President been able politically to accept such a solution, I think that he would have had the best of both worlds, but things move fast in Africa and this method was not fast enough. From the long-term point of view this is a great pity, and I think that when Nkrumah looks back in his riper years he will realise the fact.

I sometimes wonder if things could have been different—whether, somehow, I could have maintained my position, or alternatively whether my departure could have been more graceful. But I do not think so, for several reasons. The tour of the East had had a short-term, profoundly emotional effect on Nkrumah, which made him feel in a hurry to do things which his left wing friends advocated. He wanted to play a prominent part in establishing an African High Command. His partners in this concept had made it clear to him that the presence of imperialist officers in Accra was a serious handicap to this ambition. To maintain my own position, I would have had to sacrifice principles—principles which as a soldier I have had drilled into me. I could not bring myself to do so—maybe politicians find this easier.

I wonder, too, if the communists are really in fact doing so well. With the African the saying applies that 'the truth will win in the end'. The Russians do well in the short term by trying to please, regardless of whether the request makes sense. For example, the IL-18s provided for Ghana Airways have proved themselves to be far less economical to run than Western-produced aircraft. I believe that many of them now sit on the runway doing nothing. In Guinea, the Russians and, I suggest, Sékou Touré have had a shock. In the Congo, the Russians have not done nearly as well as they had hoped. Nkrumah is very unsure of himself, particularly within his own country. In spite of the flattery and pernicious propaganda poured into his ear, I still believe that with careful, diplomatic handling he may yet realise that the wicked imperialists are not as wicked as they appear to be, and the Russians and Chinese not as honest as they seem.

What, then, can we do other than adopt a negative policy in Africa? I believe that a great deal more could be done to explain to leaders like Nkrumah Britain's policy towards Africa: what we are trying to do and above all, what are our difficulties

—particularly in a country like Southern Rhodesia. At first, they may smell a rat—particularly when close advisers look for the rat—but if we go on explaining for long enough then some hopeful results should accrue. I think, again, that the press would do better to look for the good things happening in countries like Ghana rather than the bad. Of course, it is true that Nkrumah has interned a very large number of people, some quite inoffensive. Life to the African is of much less value than to the European and Nkrumah feels himself threatened—and he would have good reason for being frightened if he did not rule with an iron hand. Recent events in East Africa must have further convinced him of this. It is terribly sad that people are afraid to speak, but let us hope that with increasing age the President will become more paternal and less ruthless. In any case, nothing which the British press says is likely to change his policy—it is much more likely to make him more ruthless.

On the credit side, by comparison with the United Kingdom for example, one can see that vicious crime in Ghana is insignificant. Nepotism is no greater, and the labour relations between employer and employee are better than they are in Britain. It would, of course, be wrong to say that Ghana at the present time is an entirely happy country; nor am I very sure that the United Kingdom is, either. I feel quite certain that, given time, countries like Ghana will 'sort themselves out'. We have been through the period of arbitrary power and of confining our enemies to the Tower: Ghana is now going through that period.

We can, however, take more constructive action to help our relations with the new countries of Africa. The leaders are all very proud of being leaders and we should not show reluctance in giving them the 'red carpet' treatment when they visit this country. They are certainly given it when they visit the East and it makes a big impression on them. Although we say that military aid is a waste of money, newly independent countries will insist on having armies and we can do more financially to help train their armed forces and make it easier for them to buy military equipment from the West. We can do more, also, to take greater numbers of their officer cadets for training in this country at a lower cost. After all, the Russians were willing to accept 400 overnight. Soviet bloc countries pay great attention to visits to their part of the world by the youth of these young countries and subsidise such visits. The youth of today will be the leaders of tomorrow and I feel that we should do more on the same lines. I think also that we could retain our trading position in Africa if we were more ready to grant easy term loans. In newly independent African countries we have to face the fact that, whether or not the efficiency of their armed forces suffers, they want to see African officers in charge. We must speed up the training of such officers. After all, Ghana was the most advanced in this respect and yet progress was considered too slow.

9   The difficulties of an expatriate Chief of Defence Staff in a newly independent African state

WHEN I first went to Ghana I had no idea that some of the actions which I would be called upon to carry out as President Nkrumah's Chief of Defence Staff would almost enter the realm of fantasy. It is difficult for people in Western countries to understand the position in which a commander finds himself when serving an African left wing leader. When I received my briefing in the War Office and in the Commonwealth Relations' Office before departing for Ghana, my task was summarised as being to train Ghana's armed forces and to try to ensure that plans for their expansion remained within the realm of reality. This seemed a reasonably sensible and simple task because I imagined that, when I gave military advice, this would be taken in good faith and that I would not find myself embroiled in African politics. But I soon found that I was wrong. Very early in our association, Nkrumah made it clear to me what he wanted: an army of divisional size equipped with all the modern weapons of war, an air force which contained two squadrons of jet fighters, and a large navy and a new naval base. That the money did not exist to pay for all this mattered not one jot; that the expansion could not be produced overnight or in any case achieved efficiently without slowing up the Africanisation of the officer corps were arguments brushed aside. His target date for completion was 1962. The Russians produced a paper advocating armed services of approximately this shape and leading Nkrumah to believe that it could all be effected very quickly; therefore, said the extremists, it could only be imperialist intrigue which was stopping Nkrumah from achieving his aim.

As if these difficulties were not enough I found myself embroiled frequently when Nkrumah or Ghana were in trouble, particularly in the Congo. For example, it is hardly the task of a Chief of Defence Staff personally to rescue an ambassador like Welbeck who finds himself in a dangerous position of his own making.

Whenever suspicion arose that Ghana's military contingent was about to act outside the United Nations, I had to explain to Nkrumah that this was not possible. Either his contingent must be allowed to conform to the orders issued by the United Nations military command or he would have to withdraw it from the Congo. However, there is this to be said to Nkrumah's credit: he was the one and only leader of a country belonging to the Casablanca bloc who kept his contingent in the Congo after the Casablanca conference. This decision of his must have required great courage, and when he stepped from his aeroplane on his return to Accra from Casablanca, Nkrumah said to me: 'I fought like a lion.'

When a country such as Ghana is pursuing policies, many of which one knows to be contrary to the interests of one's parent country, there is bound to be a mental conflict of loyalties. I often found it very difficult to act on Nkrumah's orders without feeling that I might be hurting British interests.

One or two little stories illustrate the peculiar situations which could arise. Nkrumah had told me that he wished the army intelligence system to be strengthened. When I arrived in Ghana it was practically non-existent. I set about training and strengthening the organisation, and thanks to this, I heard that a consignment of arms from the East had been unloaded at Takoradi port. I had been told nothing about this and was naturally disturbed, because I did not know how these arms were to be used. My uneasiness was nothing to the consternation of the Americans and British. I received a message from the Americans asking if I knew anything about the rumours circulating in Accra. My answer was that if the Americans were worried they had better approach Nkrumah, because any import of arms from the East that might have taken place was not of my doing. At eleven o'clock the following morning, I was sent for by the President; he showed me an *aide-memoire* from the American ambassador, enquiring about the rumours and asking particularly whether it was intended that some of these weapons should be sent on to Gizenga in Stanleyville. Nkrumah, with a sweet smile, said to me: 'Of course the rumour is true, General, but I did not like to tell you of my intentions because I knew that you would not approve. They are not necessarily earmarked to go to Gizenga, but I had to accept a stockpile of these weapons as part of the price for keeping my contingent in the Congo; you had better draft a suitable reply to the American ambassador, telling him to mind his own business.'

So I found myself drafting a reply of which I still have the original!

On another occasion, I had been playing polo one afternoon, and as I left the polo ground my driver and car appeared. In the back he had my uniform. He said, 'The President wishes you to meet him at the airport immediately.' I wondered vaguely whether some revolution had broken out and if Nkrumah was fleeing the country. I hurried to Joe Michel's house, which is on the way to the airport, and there I changed.

It was dark by the time I reached the airfield and I had some difficulty in finding the President. Eventually I discovered him beside a very smart-looking VIP aeroplane called a 'Grumman Gulf Stream'. The President said: 'This is a lovely aeroplane, General, and I think we should have it.'

There were already eight various types of aircraft in the small Ghana Airways, and the Ghana air force had quite as many aircraft, either delivered or on order, to keep them busy for some time. So I was not particularly keen to take on one more different type. All the same, there was nothing for it but to inspect the aeroplane.

It was a really smart aircraft fitted out for VIP travel and had a good range—some 2,500 miles, I think. All I could do at the time was to fight a delaying action until I could find some air force officers to reinforce my arguments against having the Grumman. As both the travelling salesman and the local agent were present, I suggested we might have a trial flight the next morning to test the aircraft's flying and landing capabilities. This was agreed and the following morning Air Commodore Whitworth, Wing-Commander Gundry-White and I set off on a trial trip to Takoradi.

On the way to Takoradi the aircraft flew quite normally and it did a good landing on arrival. On the way back we decided that something would have to be done to prove to the local agent that the aircraft did not give as smooth a ride as everyone might think. Gundry-White and I took over the controls, and by the time we had finished our very erratic aerobatics the local agent was prostrate on the floor of the aircraft. When finally we landed back at Accra, he stepped from the Grumman, touched the ground with his hand, and said: 'General, I have never been so pleased in my life to touch the earth. I shall never fly with you again.'

To cut a long story short, I again saw the President and advised against buying the aircraft, mainly because of the cost of purchase and maintenance and because it was yet another different type. The President agreed that we need not have it, but I found that someone had signed a 'bill of intent'. Luckily, the 'application for purchase' had now to go through the Ministry of Defence, and by keeping this particular document in my safe for two months or so, I hoped and prayed that I had killed the purchase. It had not arrived by the time I left Ghana.

The defence committee, chaired by the President, had long agreed that the Caribou aircraft, a very short take-off type produced in Canada, was the best large transport for the small Ghana air force. Several had been ordered. I had known for some time that the Russian ambassador had been pressing Nkrumah to purchase more IL-18s and another military aircraft called the NA-12. I suspected that his motive was a Russian footing in the Ghana air force, for the small force had not the trained manpower for either manning or maintenance. So I resisted this suggestion.

One morning Erica Powell, Nkrumah's British personal assistant, rang me up and told me that the President wished me to take delivery of two IL-18s and one NA-12. I do not know exactly what I said to Erica, but I asked to see Nkrumah immediately. She replied that at the moment he had an ambassador with him (I remarked that I was quite certain he had!). I hurried to Flagstaff House and waited for the Russian ambassador to emerge. As he came out he looked surprised to see me and said: 'General, what brings you here?'

I replied somewhat brusquely: 'You should know.'

Upon seeing Nkrumah I explained again the main arguments against taking on more types of aeroplanes in the Ghana air force. With a sweet smile he answered: 'General, if you do not want the aeroplanes you need not have them', which seemed to end that one.

I am told that later in the day Krobo Edusei, the Ghanaian minister of Transport, was told to take them into Ghana Airways: at any rate there were a good many members of Ghana Airways cursing me for some time after the event.

One more story. During the course of my stay in Ghana, I had formed a President's Guard company, whose main duty was to guard Flagstaff House and visiting VIPs. It made Congo reliefs simpler, and found a home for old soldiers unfit for active service. Not long before I left Ghana I was sent for by Mr de Graft Dickson, who was then the minister of Defence, and told that the President wanted the Guards to be taught the Russian goose-step. On top of this they were to wear Russian-type jackboots. My service in Ghana had taught me to be surprised at nothing, so I merely asked who was to teach them the drill. 'Send an officer to Moscow to learn it', said de Graft Dickson.

Having slept on this extraordinary request, I returned to the attack by suggesting that if the President wished his Guard to dress and act in the Russian fashion this was his right, but it might be more politic to leave the change until after the Queen's impending visit. In any case it would be a bit complicated if one section of his small army had drill different to the majority. These arguments were not well received, but I managed to stall, and nothing constructive happened before I left Ghana. For all I know, the Guard company are now sweating it out in Russian jackboots and goose-stepping up and down the drive of Flagstaff House.

One day I had a rather amusing interview with the Yugoslav ambassador. The Yugoslavs had been commissioned to build a new naval base for the Ghana navy, and I was told to assist them in any way I could during their initial planning. We had Royal Naval officers and Royal Engineers who had knowledge of this particular location and could have assisted them. I therefore went to see the Yugoslav ambassador to find out exactly what assistance he would like to have. To start with he was very antagonistic and implied that he did not wish to have any assistance from the British and would make do with such Ghanaian assistance as was forthcoming. Tactfully, I tried to explain to him that the practical and technical knowledge could be produced only by seconded British officers. I was not doing very well until the ambassador leaned forward to stress a point and at that stage of the proceedings his bow tie fell off. I bent down, picked it up and returned it to him. He could not resist bursting out laughing and from then on our interview went quite amicably.

We in the Ministry of Defence used to say that unless there were at least two crises a week, something was wrong. This turned out to be quite true, because during my last fortnight in Ghana there were no crises. At the end of the fortnight I was sacked.

The officers and Ministry of Defence had to be pretty versatile in juggling their financial figures and organisational charts, because new units were apt to be dreamed up overnight. In May 1961, I attended a durbar at Tamale, where Nkrumah saw a number of northern horsemen perform. He was apparently so struck by their performance that at a subsequent speech to the troops on the same day, he declared, 'I have decided to form a cavalry squadron.' He then told me to design the uniform, and that the squadron must be trained in time for the Queen to see. This was done, largely due to the efforts of Major Dacres Dickson, but where the money came from I have yet to discover.

Throughout the innumerable crises and extraordinary requests, the main requirement was to keep a sense of humour. Events such as dining with a Russian president and escorting him round a Guard of Honour, co-operating with the Yugoslavs in the construction of a naval base, evolving plans for supplying arms to Gizenga and invasion plans against various 'friendly territories'—all this certainly kept people on their toes. Nkrumah is a man in a hurry: if he wants helicopters he wants them at once; if he wants a new barracks he wants it yesterday. So life is never dull.

I remember shortly after the 'Welbeck Affair' Colonel Harry Coates, the American military attaché, said to me: 'It looks to me, General, as if you have got away with it this time, but one day they'll get you in a hole from which you cannot get out.' What he said turned out to be only too true.

In Ghana, nothing but the biggest and best is good enough. But the standards employed are sometimes a little naïve. The Boeing 707 is better than a Comet; it is better because it makes more noise, and also it is bigger; therefore it is preferred, quite irrespective of whether it can be operated economically or not. It was like being in an old nursery fairytale. The situation was always being aggravated by the presence of the 'wicked uncle' (the Russians) who were whispering in the receptive ear that the 'good fairy', or the adviser, was being mean and trying to trick the 'babes in the wood'. I am of the firm opinion that although some of the military advice which I gave to Nkrumah became more and more unpalatable, the type of advice which the Russians produced must in the long term rebound, and 'wicked uncles', after all, usually come to a sticky end.

I think that it would now be worth while to go slightly more fully into this subject of loyalty, to discuss whether it is possible under present circumstances for a senior expatriate to hold a high post in a newly independent country of Africa without finding himself in an impossible position. In my case the position was complicated by the fact that the beliefs and views of President Nkrumah, the United Kingdom government and the United Nations in the Congo were often widely divergent. In the case of the Congo, the formula which I adopted was fairly simple. I felt that I must support the United Nations when I was in the Congo, at the same time striving to save Ghana's 'face' whenever this became necessary; although at times I certainly did not agree with British attitudes, these were no affair of mine.

Even this simple formula sometimes led me into difficulties. For example, a very fine Sudanese called Mekki Abbas took over the post of head civil United Nations representative for a short period after the departure of Mr Dayal (a high Indian civil servant). It was during a time when the United Nations military command were in grave difficulties due to the withdrawal of many military contingents from the Congo, including the powerful Moroccan contingent. At a meeting in Casablanca of various African countries—Ghana, Morocco, Guinea, Mali, the UAR, the Algerian FLN and Libya—one of the decisions arrived at was that the participating powers so disapproved of United Nations actions in the Congo that they would withdraw their contingents. Ghana alone dissented. The Casablanca powers were, of course, mainly extreme Pan-African, and their policies were opposed by another group of African powers, who can be called the Brazzaville group—mainly French-speaking. Although Nkrumah had bravely decided to leave his contingent in the Congo he was under constant pressure to change this decision and he repeatedly discussed this subject with me. In my view it was in his own interests, as a 'neutralist' loyally supporting the United Nations, to leave his contingent in the Congo, and it would also have been a severe blow to the United Nations had he withdrawn it at that particular time. I therefore used all the influence I could to persuade him to stick to his decision. On one of my visits to the Congo I passed through Leopoldville and paid a courtesy call on Mekki Abbas. During the course of our conversation he asked me two main questions. The first was whether President Nkrumah was likely to leave his contingent in the Congo. My reply was that I thought so, and that I would use all the influence I could to persuade him to do so. The second concerned a rumour that Nkrumah intended to fly arms into Stanleyville for Gizenga. Was this true? My answer to this one was that the President had certainly been toying with the idea—he had a supply of Russian arms in Ghana which could be used for this purpose—but the physical difficulties of refuelling aircraft were so great that, unless he could obtain refuelling rights at Khartoum, such action would be extremely difficult and could in any case only be on a very small scale. I agreed with Mekki Abbas that any action of this kind would only aggravate an extremely difficult situation, and said I had already explained to Nkrumah the doubtful wisdom of doing anything of this nature.

At the end of our conversation, Mekki Abbas seemed a good deal happier, and I thought no more about the interview. Some two weeks later, in Accra, I was suddenly sent for by the President. He produced a message from New York which was a report of my conversation with Mekki Abbas and included some of the points I had made. I had, of course, to admit that I had had such conversation, but it was awkward. Were my actions right or wrong? Had I been disloyal to Nkrumah? The question of whether or not arms should be sent to Gizenga presented me with another conflict in loyalty. My advice to Nkrumah throughout was always against such action, largely on the grounds that it would not help the United Nations to produce a satisfactory solution and would only lead to further unnecessary bloodshed in the Congo. I am certain that this advice was in the interests of United Nations efforts, but I sometimes found it hard to argue when I knew perfectly well that Tshombe and Kalonji were receiving arms from Western sources.

In the middle of 1960, I knew that a Russian military mission had arrived in Ghana, and of course was somewhat perturbed. When I tackled President Nkrumah, he was evasive and said that although he did not intend to use Russian instruction or weapons, it was nice to have the views of a large military power on the training of his armed forces. It was, of course, not very nice for me and perhaps I should have asked him whether he trusted me to do my best for him or whether he would prefer that the Russians do their best for him. I did go so far as to say that he must realise that the Russians' report was unlikely to be favourable so far as I was concerned, since they could hardly be very pleased to see an 'imperialist' general in my position.

When the report came out it was, of course, critical of all the British training and organisational methods, and was gravely dishonest in what it advocated as possible. The expansion recommended was out of all proportion to the national resources available to Ghana, but the list of tanks, guns, aircraft and other equipment must have looked attractive to the African dreamer. It would be interesting to know what the British Chief of the General Staff would do if he heard that the American Chiefs of Staff had been asked to examine the organisation and training of the British army and say whether they thought that the Army Board was doing its job properly.

The pressure to send large numbers of officer cadets to Russia for training presented an almost more complex problem. It was in the interests neither of Nkrumah himself nor, certainly, of the United Kingdom that this should take place. From the point of view of Nkrumah, he would be in danger of having half his army Russian orientated and the other half anti-Russian orientated. I cannot believe that the Russian military schools where these boys have gone will preclude any political indoctrination. From the British point of view it was unpleasant to think that a lot of good little communists were being trained to take their place in Nkrumah's army. However, it was not necessary for me to get involved in the political aspects of such a decision. It was enough for me that, from the purely military angle, mixed training, mixed arms, mixed equipment, mixed transport and mixed techniques make for military nonsense.

When President Nkrumah received a large consignment of Russian arms, what was I to do? As his Chief of Defence Staff I would, under normal circumstances, have expected to have been consulted and also to have had some inkling of how it was intended to use such arms. As it was, I came to know of their arrival from my own sources of information and was never told how these weapons were to be used, although I had a pretty shrewd idea.

At one time it was decided that a foreign country should build a naval base for the Ghana navy. Not only was this an unnecessary luxury but the terms of the agreement were very unfavourable to Ghana. However, both I and the British naval commander found it difficult to explain matters without coming under suspicion of being against the scheme purely because it was being carried through by a communist country. When President Nkrumah kept on buying more and more Russian turbo-prop aircraft he suspected that my argument against such aircraft was largely because they were Russian, whereas, of course, this was untrue. The true reason was that Ghana already had more than enough aircraft on her hands.

I also had to face the unpleasantness of the British being accused of responsibility for the death of both Lumumba and Hammarskjold. Such accusations were made to my face, and were hard to bear placidly.

Throughout the period of the Congo crisis, Nkrumah was under constant political pressure to withdraw all the British officers from the Ghana contingent. From his point of view this would, politically, have been a good move, but I could not accede to it if he wished to retain a sizeable contingent in the

Congo. The troops themselves would have suffered from lack of leadership, lack of administration and, in many cases, their lives would have been in jeopardy. Many people in Western circles were amazed that I said that I thought the proposed African High Command a good thing. I still think that it is a good thing. It will take a very long time to set up such a High Command efficiently; language difficulties, differences in training, in organisation and in national characteristics all contribute to making the process slow, but it is a logical process if it can be kept on a neutralist level.

The preceding paragraphs only scratch the surface of the difficulties which must face an expatriate serving in a country such as Ghana, and I think one can tackle the problem only after establishing for oneself certain guiding principles. I like to think that my guiding principle with Nkrumah was that, however much it might hurt, honesty was the only possible policy. The Russian policy seems to be that anything is possible, but I am sure this will boomerang in the end. One must not forget that something which Nkrumah might think a good idea one day became a bad idea three days later, after he had talked to somebody else. Therefore consistency and honesty in one's recommendations to him were surely the best, although I believe that in the end it was bound to mean one's own undoing. I think there were two things which riled him most: my insistence that expansion of his armed services could not proceed at the rate he wished, at the same time as rapid Africanisation; and my pointing out his blindness to the impossibility of mixing free Russian weapons with existing weapons from the West. He certainly did not like it when I consistently refused to withdraw all the British officers from the Congo, nor was he at all pleased at the strength of my resistance to cadets' going to Russia for training. In the present context of Africa, consistent honesty is bound to have an eroding effect on the position of the person concerned and I knew that it was touch and go whether I would last even two years. Shortly before my departure I predicted to a well known journalist, Colin Legum, that I would in fact be removed when Nkrumah came back from Russia. So I was not unprepared.

Finally, the most unpleasant part of life in Ghana was the feeling of fear and mistrust which existed. Very few Ghanaians were prepared to speak to you honestly, largely because they feared for their own positions. Nor was it possible ever to know exactly whom you could trust; this made everyone very guarded in conversation and the feeling always persisted that anything you said could be misinterpreted to Nkrumah.

10 Tribalism, nationalism, communism, and the drift to where?

WHAT is an African? What is a Congolese? What is a Ghanaian? What is a Kenyan? What are the motives driving the various established and emerging leaders in Africa today? Is it hate for the former colonial or existing colonial master? Is it the desire to get one's own back on the former oppressor? Is it lust for power? Is it genuine nationalism, wishing to build a nation? Are many of the emerging African leaders steeped in communist doctrines and convinced that the communist way of life is the answer for them? Have they been converted by their VIP treatment when they visited communist countries and disappointed by their reception during similar visits to the West? What part does tribalism still play in the African context? Is it dead, and can in fact the black African build a united nation overnight?

This is the kind of question which one finds discussed on television, in books and in the national press; they are all hard questions to answer. I would not presume to think that I could give an answer to any of them, but I might venture to give a few comments on some of the factors which go to make up this jig-saw puzzle. I think it would be true to say that there are very few black 'Africans'. Even Nkrumah, who in many ways must be as near 'African', as opposed to Ghanaian, as anyone, retains many of his tribal suspicions. His closest body-guard come from his own tribe; he suspects certain tribes in Ghana; he has broken, or thinks he has broken, the power of the tribal chiefs in Ghana—not because he no longer believes in tribalism, but because the tribal chiefs were against him. There are very few, if any, Africans whom you can classify as such and who do not still retain tribal loyalties. For the majority the priority of loyalty is, I think, as follows: first, the tribe; second, self; third, the nation; fourth, a love-hate towards the old colonial rule; and fifth, a sneaking admiration for the power of Russia and communist methods.

Ghana is not a good example to go by because it is relatively small. Provided that the army and the police remain loyal to Nkrumah, he should have little difficulty in dealing with any particular tribe, and in a small country like this, with small tribes, tribal feeling is not likely to be so intense. The former Belgian Congo gives a far better example of the pattern in Africa. It will be many years before the Baluba, the Luntu and the Lulua will live in harmony as Congolese. They do not regard themselves as Congolese, but as members of their tribes; for this very reason, although sentimental politicians like to think of strong countries united by geography, it will be a long time before anything better than loose federalism can work, certainly in the larger countries. Anti-colonialism is a queer mixture; it is a mixture of wishing to have a whipping boy to blame for the troubles through which newly independent countries must pass (due largely to the sudden drop in administrative efficiency, because the African cannot yet do things as well as his former master), and a sort of adolescent love-hate.

It is probably true to say that many of the whites living in Africa today are better 'Africans' than the black African. This is understandable. The white 'African' has in the past been the 'have', whereas the black African has been the 'have not'. Many generations of education have made it possible for the white 'African' to organise and do things better than the black man. The former does not wish to see graft and greed creep into the affairs of his country. Further, in many cases his methods are more honest and more genuinely in the national interest than those of the black African. Nevertheless the wind of change cannot be stopped—nor can the fall in efficiency. If the white man

is to stay in Africa, he will have to accept a less efficient government and temporary increase in incompetence. Black Africans
are not going to wait seventy years or so until the white minority
consider them fit to run their own affairs. In many areas there
will be a reversion back to stronger tribalism before nationalism
emerges again.

In my own view, communism as such stands a real chance
only in areas where the white man fights to the death to retain
white supremacy. The African does not wish to throw off one
alien ruler and creed to take on another. He will evolve his own
salvation and it will be one involving many sad growing pains.
The salvation of Africa, to my mind, lies in the fact that the vast
majority of black Africans are natural gentlemen; the minority,
some of whom are now powerful figures, are certainly not
gentlemen, but these will in time be thrust aside.

Up to the time of the Congo crisis there had been little
perceptible drift further to the left in Ghana, but this disaster
gave the anti-British and anti-Western elements sufficient head
of steam to accelerate what was probably inevitable. For reasons
best known to President Nkrumah himself, he had gradually
discarded more and more of his moderates, which meant that
the bulk of the advice given to him was poison as far as Western
policies were concerned. Why he did this is hard to say; whether
the reason was fear that their intelligence might reduce his own
power, or his wish to steer a more and more extreme course of
which he knew these advisers would not approve, is difficult to
decide. The reasons are probably a combination of the two,
allied with his firm belief that the only sure way of obtaining the
leadership in Africa was to be the most virulently anti-Western
and extremist of all. Prior to his long visit behind the Iron
Curtain in the late summer of 1960, I feel quite sure that
Nkrumah was motivated by African nationalism; and even now,
if he has been convinced that communism is the answer for his
country, it is primarily because he thinks the East will sponsor
him as the major leader in Africa; he also thinks he can use the
Russians to help him to defeat the so-called colonialists; finally,
his mind has become so saturated with the poison poured in his
ear day after day that he can no longer bring himself to believe
moderate arguments.

As I have said earlier in this book, the main motive for his actions at the beginning of the Congo crisis was to bring about a union between the Congo and Ghana, and it seemed to him that Lumumba was the one and only leader likely to agree to any such union—although in the event I do not believe Lumumba would have done so. Since the Russians backed Lumumba, though for different motives, they were Nkrumah's allies in the fight against the wicked colonialists. Whatever the motives and reasons for this drift, the drift itself became more and more apparent as the Congo crisis continued.

We who worked as servants in independent African countries had to try to think as Africans. That is to say, we had to try and look at problems from the point of view of the African, and try to analyse, not what we as British or other white men might think, but what the Ghanaian, the Congolese, and the Nigerian, etc., were thinking. In Ghana it seemed to many of us that Russia regarded Ghana as its number one target in Africa. The Russians assumed, possibly incorrectly, that Guinea was aligned in their direction, but they were not yet certain of Ghana, and they appeared to be making an effort in that country out of all proportion to the overall value of the prize. I have often asked myself why. I am now going to make an attempt to analyse the thoughts of various imaginary characters on the African scene. The thoughts and opinions may not be correct but they represent an effort to look at the problem, not from the British point of view, but from the point of view of other characters on the stage.

It was inevitable that during my stay I should come in contact with many moderate Ghanaian politicians and moderates in all walks of life. The average Ghanaian is not politically minded, nor is he particularly interested in the Convention People's Party. He is interested in being able to feed himself and his family. Even so, nearly all the poorer Ghanaians realised that something sad was happening in their country.

I think that a moderate politician thought more or less along these lines: 'Oh, my poor country; it is not what I expected when we were given the much-heralded "freedom" from colonial rule and later became a republic. There seems to be less liberty, particularly to speak one's mind, than ever there was during the time of the wicked colonialists. There are more political detainees than ever there were during the colonial days. What has gone wrong? In my heart of hearts I feel that the

British, our old colonial masters, have brought about some of this misery and some of this anti-Western pressure; but how? It seems to me that they talk too much in public, particularly those who have reactionary views, about Africa, and that some of their friends in Africa, through their public utterances, clearly play into the hands of the extremists, backed by the communists. It seems to me also that a large section of their press is irresponsible. Instead of trying to understand that our politicians are children playing a new game, based largely on the cult of the individual, they expect them to act like responsible Western politicians. When something happens not in accordance with Western standards, the press in the United Kingdom and America becomes hysterical. It is often argued by them that our press is terrible, untruthful and biased, receiving much of its material from Eastern sources. This is probably true and I myself do not like our press, but is it any excuse for a so-called major power, with years of experience in journalism, to descend to the same level? I think that possibly the West is sometimes vulnerable to the criticism that she approaches many of her problems in Africa from the financial point of view—that is to say, that she is most sensitive when her financial interests seem to be threatened—although I may be wrong. I realise that the standard of living of the British people depends upon Britain's retaining its existing overseas markets and on being able to trade, but in the long term I would have thought that Britain is much more likely to retain these markets if, in the Congo for example, it follows a policy which is in the interests of the country concerned, rather than in the interests of outsiders. I wonder also whether sometimes the West does not take too much trouble over the trouble makers and does not pay enough attention to helping the moderates. The average African new leader is out for what he can get from either East or West, and if one or two of them think it is of benefit to align themselves closely with the East in order to get financial and other aid, the West should not try to compete in an out-bidding contest, but rather try to put its money into places where moderation and true 'neutralism' rule the day. Some say that before long there will be no moderates left ruling the new countries of Africa, but I consider this to be a passing phase. In Ghana, the British seemed to have bent over backwards to placate Nkrumah when his official newspapers, which I know can print only what he himself sanctions, poured out lies about the British. This will not pay in the long term, because people like Nkrumah will think that they can get away with anything and still receive aid from the West. A policy of firmness but fairness towards newly independent African countries may mean that the West loses out temporarily in some areas, but I am quite certain that in the long term this policy would produce nothing but gain. The West as a whole seems inclined to confuse communism with African nationalism. Surely no one imagines that the Russians or the Chinese are going to get away with 'colonising' the African territories; if they do try to do so the stage might be reached where the country concerned would turn to the West for assistance against them. Has this not happened already in East Africa? We may have our extremists but they are mostly extreme nationalists, not pro-communists. The danger in Africa seems to me to be the growth of anti-Western feeling, not the growth of communism. The inability of some Westerners to understand that 'the wind of change' cannot now be halted and the reluctance of some Western countries to face up to the risks of giving independence, produces a natural alignment between the Pan-African and the communist. This will kill trade for the West far more effectively than any direct action by the Russians or other communists. From what I have seen of the Russians, they are not particularly adept at understanding the African, but they possess the advantage of being prepared to flatter when flattery pays and are in the enviable position of being able to encourage anti-colonialism.'

Now let us turn to the thoughts of a moderate Congolese politician during the early phases of the Congo crisis: 'What a mess! I am frightened. I am frightened of three things: first, my soldiers—they are savages and little has been done to bring them under control; secondly, the intentions of the Russians and Chinese—I fear that they wish to capture through chaos the riches of the Congo, most of which should be spent in this country for the benefit of the Congolese people; thirdly, I am frightened of Western intentions. Do the people of the West not realise that we cannot be without Katanga and a proportion of its wealth? Do they not realise that Britain, by its seeming hostility to the United Nations, might force the Congolese central government to align itself more and more with the East?

I am worried about the ineffectiveness of the United Nations. Why did they not establish law and order and bring our savage soldiers under control? Why do various countries, who said that they were friendly towards us and wished to establish a stable Congo, withdraw their military assistance at a time when we most need it? This was not a friendly act. Why have the Western politicians so often been mistrustful of the intentions of UN officials? Do they not realise the difficulties with which these men have to compete? Do they not realise that the East is continually trying to undermine the United Nations' efforts to restore law and order? The withdrawal of military contingents is but one example. How can the United Nations be expected to help us if both the East and the West oppose any progress? What do the Russians and Chinese want in the Congo at this moment? It seems to me that they want continued chaos, so that normal trade remains at a standstill and the plantations and mines and so on collapse in ruins. This will not only hurt the Congolese; it will hurt the West. What does the West want? I can only assume that they want stability to be able to trade. This stability will be produced only by backing the United Nations. Wherever United Nations contingents have been stationed, there peace reigns and people can go about their work unmolested. Of course we are intolerably childish as politicians—we have not been trained—but we prefer to deal with the headmaster, the United Nations, rather than be continually interfered with by the ex-colonial nannies. Let these nannies stop interfering inside the school, the Congo; if they object to anything taking place they should represent it properly at the board of governors, the United Nations secretariat. I sometimes think, although I do not agree with the policies followed by President Nkrumah towards the Congo, there was much to be said for his plea that all ambassadors should be withdrawn from Leopoldville until a central government had been firmly established with UN assistance.'

Now let us try to analyse the thoughts of a Russian ambassador in an African country: 'Ah! Africa—let us have a brief look at the board. How are we doing there? On the whole, I do not think we are doing too badly, although we have had our disappointments. I think that we are not doing too badly because we know what we want. What is it we want? We do not, at this stage, wish to convert the people of Africa to communism—they are too immature to understand communism. What we do want is to convert a few key figures in each country clearly to our side and to anti-Westernism. This latter is our policy towards Ghana. Elsewhere, such as in the Congo, we wish chaos to continue, thereby making the Congo a financial drain on the West instead of being a financial asset. In fact, our major aims in Africa are economic—to stop Western trade and therefore to help to undermine the capitalist system. Let us look at Ghana for a moment: is it worth the effort we are putting in? After all, it is only a small country. It is not very rich—in fact, it is now poor—but on the other hand it was the first country in Africa to be granted independence by the British. Furthermore, Nkrumah as a revolutionary leader has great emotional appeal amongst the disruptive elements both in the free countries of Africa and in the remaining colonies and South Africa. I think, also, that we could use Ghana as a base for operations elsewhere —that is, a place from which to feed weapons into other countries, and in which to give subversive instruction to revolutionary elements from elsewhere, similar to the use to which we hope to put Cuba. This being the case, what shall we do? Our first job is to capture Nkrumah by flattery—I think he will fall for this. We must also help to discredit his moderates by producing evidence that they are corrupt and disloyal to him. We must get political control of the army, the last stronghold of Commonwealth feeling. We can do this last by offering free weapons and military training in Russia for their young men. But we must not forget that Nkrumah is unreliable so far as we are concerned. It is doubtful whether he is a true communist—he is certainly dedicated to keeping himself in power and we must get him into a position either from which there is no retreat for him or from which it is possible for us to remove him. I think that at the moment he still believes he is clever enough to steer his own course. We will see. Next, what about the Congo? Is it important and if so, what is the score? One has only to look at the map of Africa to realise that geographically it is of the greatest importance. Continued chaos here is bound to have its effect on neighbouring countries. Economically it is not really important to us, but it is to the West. How are things going here? I think they are touch-and-go. At one time it looked as though we were out, and we have certainly had our set-backs, but we have a chance if the American course of backing the central government in Leopoldville does not succeed. If the West places too many obstacles in the way of a solution between Leopoldville and Katanga, then we have a chance of promoting continued chaos. It suited us that the United Nations operations, both in the civilian and military field, should be restricted in their effectiveness. Luckily, the West has done this job for us.'

Lastly, let us try to analyse the thoughts of an unfortunate senior United Nations official in the Congo: 'If I stay here much longer, I shall go mad. What happens in the Congo is completely out of this world and sometimes the lack of understanding displayed by Western diplomatists appals me. Will people not realise that Congolese politicians are immature and quite unpredictable, that in common with most African politicians a written agreement reached round a conference table in all probability means no more than pleasing those present. Like the trades unions in Britain, as soon as one agreement is reached they then start to study how to squeeze a little more juice out of the lemon. Will people also not realise that the only way to save the Congo from Eastern domination is by producing a solution which at least nominally puts Katanga under the central government? What is this talk about certain sections of the Congolese army being more reliable than other sections? There are, of course, units in the Katanga, Stanleyville and Leopoldville which are better disciplined than others, but very few can be relied upon not to commit murder or rape once they have taken drink. Further, unless and until these armies are brought under effective control law and order in the Congo will never become established. It is no use condemning communistic or left-wing African aid for Gizenga and Lumumbists when aid of all kinds has been streaming in to Tshombe and Kalonji, almost unstopped. If you condone mercenaries working in Tshombe's army who have no responsibility for co-operating with United Nations, surely it is logical that the East should be allowed to send military officers to Stanleyville. Militarily we are now too weak to be effective throughout the whole of the Congo. This is what the communists wanted, and the West has done little to build up confidence in the United Nations military command. Unless Katanga can be persuaded to adhere to some agreements with Leopoldville, the latter government will probably turn to the East, because even in Adoula's cabinet there are some extremist Pan-Africans. It is all right in London to talk about "peaceful negotiations". In an atmosphere of anarchy peace has to be enforced. Time is certainly running out.'

11   The future

'I have made a ceaseless effort not to ridicule, not to bewail,
nor to scorn human actions, but to understand them.'

Spinoza.

WHAT of the future in Ghana, and other newly independent
African countries? Tim McCabe, who used to work in Ghana's
Special Branch, and I often talked about the future. He was
inclined to be a pessimist and say that the West has lost out in
Africa because of its failure to understand the problem and
understand the African. I am not so despondent. Undoubtedly
Russia and China are making an all out effort in Africa and this
effort will continue. As I have said earlier I do not believe that
they are necessarily making an all out effort to convert Africa to
communism, and history has shown that the use or threat of
force seems to be necessary to introduce a communist regime,
particularly if that regime is to turn the country into a satellite.
I am convinced that their effort is more to oust the West economically in order, eventually, to undermine the capitalist system
as a whole. Although on the surface the West does not appear to
have done all that well in Africa, the Russians have weaknesses
which are already beginning to tell against them. They are
intolerant of the seeming inefficiency of the African workman
and politician. Although Nkrumah and other African politicians
are men in a hurry, the people of Africa as a whole are in no
such hurry, and the Russians find it difficult to conceal their
disgust at the inefficiency and lethargy of many Africans with
whom they have to work. Our colonial past has given us the

advantage of realising that in the African climate you cannot expect results as quickly as you can in the more temperate climates of the north.

By and large, the Russian is not at home in Africa—he is homesick, keeps himself very much to himself, either because it is directed so from above or because he does not understand the African; he has no real contact with the African. If this continues it will, of course, prejudice their hopes of further progress. The Russian does not really understand the African at all. He fails to understand that his failure to fulfil promises, his dishonest dealing and neglect of the truth in order to undermine the West will rebound in the end. Military cadets who go to Russia may come back as good little communists, but, in spite of Russian promises, they will not be flying IL-18s in six months. Nor have the IL-18s proved the great economic proposition which the Russians promised. By and large the African is used to reasonably honest dealing from his ex-colonial master, even if sometimes this honesty is unpleasant, and although he himself may indulge in some sharp practice, he does not expect it from European countries.

The weakness of the Western case in Africa springs partly from emotionalism. The emotional support by the United States for anti-colonialism has borne fruit and it has meant that many countries are liable to get their independence before they are ready for it. It is too late now to turn back the pages of history; to do so would only make matters worse. The ex-colonial powers in Africa must suffer for a few years and realise that each country, as it becomes free, is liable for the time being to turn on the ex-colonial master. If we are patient I think these countries will come to realise that the ex-colonial master is really not so bad when he compares him with the alternatives, and many of them, President Nkrumah included, may find that it is better to deal with 'the devil you know than the devil you don't know'.

Our biggest handicap over this difficult period in Africa may well prove to be the diehard, both in Africa and in this country, who fails to realise that, however unfortunate it may be that the 'wind of change' is becoming a hurricane, it is impossible to put the weather-vane back. All we can do is to face up to our responsibilities in the various countries concerned and not be afraid to stand firm in slowing up the hurricane if this is necessary and justifiable. The Belgian Congo was, to my mind, an example of an ex-colonial power throwing away its responsibility for the sake of popularity. We must not do the same, however unpopular this makes us in the short term. The biggest nonsense ever preached in Africa was 'one man, one vote'; but the West preached it, and it means now that the rabble rouser rather than the responsible politician may well get control in newly independent countries. Herein is the quandary; should we surrender to the rabble rouser because he is supported by the virulent Pan-Africanists or should we stand firm on our responsibilities? I think we should choose the latter. It will make us unpopular in certain quarters for a short time, but we would be failing in our duty if we contributed to the chaos rather than to the stability of Africa. It is the speed of the hurricane rather than its inevitability which presents the problem.

All the time we have with us our free press, which is not always helpful to the government or helpful to the policies we are trying to pursue in Africa. When countries win their freedom we must not expect a Western pattern of democracy. One has only to be in any newly independent African country for a short time to realise that they are ready neither for 'one man, one vote' nor the Westminster type of democracy, and that a strong dictatorship is probably the best thing for some time. The men we send to serve in Africa must regard themselves as expendable, standing for the right however unpopular this may be with the government in Whitehall. It seems to me that the Africans are not alone in believing that 'safety first' is the best answer once they have reached a comfortable position. The problem is not to fight communism baldheadedly, but to come to terms with Pan-Africanism, in order to defeat the communist effort.

It is important to realise that Africa is a continent, inhabited by many different peoples. For instance, the Arab of the north, the African of the west, of the south and of central Africa are very different both in outlook and temperament. There is very little real love lost between the Arab and the true African. This means that African unity as such is still a long, long way off; the one unifying factor is the determination of African leaders to produce African rule throughout Africa. I remember that President Nkrumah had in his office a map of Africa. He started this map when he first became prime minister and we had to keep it up to date for him. It showed in different colours the countries which had been 'liberated' and those which were still colonies. In common with all the other African leaders 'liberation' was an obsession with him.

It would be true to say also that my experience of Africa has really been confined to the west and to the Congo, although during my time there I met Africans from many other parts of the continent.

If I was asked whether or not independence has brought increased happiness to the common people, my answer would be 'No', for these reasons. The standard of honesty in official circles has gone down. 'Power corrupts' and the sudden acquisition of great financial power is over-tempting for some Africans. Generally, the standard of public services has deteriorated, since there are not sufficient Africans to replace trained expatriates. In many places mistrust and fear are prevalent. Tribal warfare and tribal jealousies have got the upper hand. The cost of living has risen and political freedom as we understand it does not exist. All the same, the reasons for this state of affairs has to be appreciated before passing judgement. It was powerful elements in the West who preached 'freedom' for all peoples under colonial rule irrespective of whether these people were ready for it or not. Many of the colonial powers did little to speed up the preparation for freedom which most people could see was only round the corner. The movement towards 'freedom' cannot now be halted; it must be accepted. In this respect American, Russian and sentimental left wing policies sometimes worked hand in hand with the 'one man, one vote' and 'will of the people' dogmas. Resistance by white elements in central and southern Africa has only strengthened the vigour with which the freedom doctrine has been preached.

However unfortunate the ending of my time in Africa may have been and whatever its subsequent effects on my future, I must consider myself in many ways lucky to have had this experience. I can remember talking to the Russian ambassador at a party. We had been bathing in the sea that morning. He said to me: 'General, I noticed you in the troubled waters this morning.' (That was, in the rough sea.) 'You will notice that I swam out beyond the troubled waters and remained in the calm waters. I adopt the policy of waiting in the calm waters and plunging into the troubled waters when they need stirring up.' This, of course, was easy for a communist to do, and in fact was a very good metaphor.

Maybe after these experiences one could become cynical. During them I certainly suffered periods of complete exhaustion and depression, but the funny thing was that I always did have, and still have, a burning desire to help find solutions in that continent. The enthusiasm of the African, even if sometimes misdirected, is infectious.

Also, I regard it as a privilege to have seen the United Nations personalities operating under the appalling difficulties of the Congo and was often saddened by what I thought were the seemingly obstructive attitudes of many in the West. Of course, the United Nations set-up has its weaknesses, but many of these weaknesses are due to the attitude of the great powers and are not the fault of the United Nations itself.

I am critical of some actions of the United Nations in the Congo and I think probably not without cause—the most notable occasion and the one which caused most furore was when I defended the Ghana troops against insinuations that they had failed to protect some Canadian civilians at Leopoldville airport. The unfortunate thing was that my memorandum, later published as an open document by the UN secretariat, was a personal report to President Nkrumah, not intended for publication. It was presumably attached to President Nkrumah's note to the United Nations and due to some procedural rules in the secretariat was published there as an open document. It was not intended to be a public criticism of the United Nations.

For a long time to come the mixing of communists with so-called 'imperialists' either in the secretariat of the United Nations itself or in a United Nations force, is bound to present great difficulties because few, particularly the communists, are able to owe their loyalty completely to the United Nations and to bury their national feelings. I at least know these things— that the people of Africa as a whole are peace-loving, that as civilisation is very much on the surface they are easily swayed by the rabble rouser, that the expressions 'one man, one vote' and 'will of the people' mean very little in an African context. That the way to prevent the United Nations being run by sentimental theorists is to subject it to constructive criticism and constructive support, that although we talk of the African countries as 'semi-civilised' it would be well for us to glance at both the American and British press which daily describes acts just as uncivilised as those which take place in Africa taking place in Western countries.

I see little danger of Africa's going communist. I do, however, see the danger of South African and Southern Rhodesian problems dragging on for so long that the African states unite in turning to the East for help; thereby we shall lose, politically and economically, throughout Africa. This is the one unifying factor. It will take many years for Africa to settle down; most of the existing international boundaries are falsely imposed colonial ones which will in time be sorted out. Of one thing I am certain: Africans wish to solve their own problems without dictation from anybody.

Postscript

TO understand the fantastic and immense problems facing the Africans and the West—and the East for that matter—in Africa today, one has to live there for a time. Many of the issues are largely human and we should try to be guided in our actions by what is best for the people in Africa rather than what is best for short-term power politics. The people of Africa themselves will in the event solve their own problems and they will be grateful to those countries who have helped them to do so in an unselfish manner. Whether I myself, or any of my fellow officers who served with me in Ghana, have helped Ghana or the Congo, or Africa as a whole, one cannot say. The complexity of the problem is well illustrated by the hundred and one different opinions to be read in the daily press. One or two impressions have stuck in my mind.

It seems to me, as I have said, that the problem is not the danger of these African countries going communist, but that we cannot ride out the natural wave of anti-colonialism which is at present sweeping this continent. If we cannot do so, we will lose our trade and our contacts with African countries. We must not lose in Africa because, if we do, NATO is outflanked and becomes meaningless. Sometimes I think that the whole thing is too difficult and it would be better to adopt the 'ostrich' attitude of putting one's head in the sand. I certainly would not like to go through my past experiences again, although at times I found them very interesting and even rewarding.

126

Some things stick, such as the day early in the Congo crisis when my very charming Ghanaian interpreter came to me and said that the Ghanaian ambassador had told him that if he worked any longer for me he would not get a job when he returned to Ghana, because I was an imperialist. Little instances like this were frequently happening throughout my stay in Africa, and they did wear me down.

I was impressed by the trouble communist countries took to get young men for training behind the Iron Curtain in reporting, news editing and broadcasting. As a result, many broadcasting stations and newspapers in young African countries are now controlled by communist-orientated individuals. I believe that we should do more in this direction, if it is not too late. Broadcasting and simply written newspaper articles have great impact on the large semi-educated populations, particularly if the same views are plugged hour by hour and day after day.

Running on from this is the question of radio propaganda. Radio propaganda against moderate African leaders, the 'imperialists' and the 'neo-colonialists' is poured out day by day by the Egyptians, the Russians and the Chinese. It comes from very powerful stations. The spoken word has a much greater impact in Africa than the written word and we simply must do something to counter this propaganda—again, if it is not too late.

Support for our friends in Africa is urgent. A great deal of this book was written two years or more ago. Even then the reasonably intelligent person could forecast fairly accurately the course it was feared Nkrumah was taking. Nevertheless, we have put more money into supporting him, a constant opponent of the West at least in his spoken word, than we have given to the moderates and our friends. Economic support need not be given with a flourish. It can be given quietly and surreptitiously so that, for example, the truly neutral or pro-West leaders can raise the standard of living in their countries. Very often the opposite course seems to be adopted. Those who insult us receive money to raise the standard of living in their countries, and those who support us are neglected.

The drama of Nkrumah may be drawing to its climax and I fear the result may not be a happy one. Whatever happens to Nkrumah, Ghana will still go on. Perhaps the history of what has happened in Ghana over the last three or four years will have its lessons. By being over-tolerant we may have delayed the drift towards the communist state, but we have not necessarily stopped it; had we been firmer we might have made stopping it easier. Now we must not scuttle away from the remainder of Africa. We must face up to our responsibilities, however unpopular this may make us in the short term. Above all, we must realise that the cold war is by no means ended, and that it is in fact as intense as it ever has been.

I am depressed by the blindness of some people in the West to the dangers that beset them in Africa. Do our politicians really understand the weaknesses of the communists in their struggle in Africa? Do our leaders do enough to explain to the people what is happening? If you have 'one man, one vote' and consider that people have the intelligence to use this vote, surely they should be given the facts of life by their leaders rather than platitudes? There is no doubt that, as far as my position was concerned in Ghana, the Russians held all the aces—in the short term. They were prepared to produce instructors for nothing, they were prepared to produce weapons and equipment for practically nothing. President Nkrumah was allied to Mali and Guinea, which were strongly left wing. There would never have been any shortage of Russian instructors for the armed forces, because they would have been detailed and the Russians would not have relied on volunteers, as is the British method. I was sometimes depressed by the number of people who spoke to me and said: 'General, you are doing a nice job out here, but how can it last? The Russians are working hard and have all the aces.'

Curiously enough the Russians only have a king in their hand. We hold the aces and queens if only we know how to play them.

APPENDICES

A: Record of evacuation of Mr Welbeck made at the time of the event

November 27, 1960

1. On November 20 I was ordered to go to the Congo with Richard Quarshie to investigate the evacuation order issued by Mobutu against Welbeck. I was worried because I had seen for myself the past actions of Mobutu's men. I had seen them attack and maltreat Belgian and United Nations personnel at the commencement of the operation. I knew about the forcible evacuation of the Russian and Czech embassies and did not see that Welbeck could stay in the Congo without bloodshed. I therefore went to see Adamafio on the evening of the 20th, prior to getting a final briefing from the President on Monday, the 21st. As I pointed out to the latter on the morning of November 21, there seemed to be four possible courses open to me in the negotiations with the United Nations over Welbeck's case. I explained these courses to Adamafio and that I thought I would be in a very difficult position if Welbeck should stay.

Course one was to persuade the United Nations to bring their influence to bear on Mobutu to allow Welbeck to stay, provided he had sensible advice from an experienced civil servant. This course the President authorised me to adopt.

Course two was to get the United Nations to persuade Mobutu to leave things as they were, using the threat of withdrawing the whole Ghana army if this were not agreed. I was not authorised to adopt this course.

Course three was to let Welbeck give the assurance that he would not interfere with internal politics. This course appeared impracticable and I did not ask for authority to adopt it.

The fourth course was to replace Welbeck temporarily. I pointed out to the President that unless Mobutu could be persuaded to be reasonable, this course might have to be adopted, if only as a temporary measure, unless one was prepared to accept casualties to the police and other United Nations forces. I was not authorised to adopt this course because the President said that it was up to the United Nations to curb Mobutu and further representation could be negotiated once course one had been agreed.

2.   I persuaded the Cabinet that Quarshie and I must leave on the morning of November 21, because Mobutu's ultimatum finally expired at two o'clock in the afternoon of that day. I sent a signal to Rikhye explaining to him that we were coming and that I held him to his verbal promise to me that Welbeck would be protected by the United Nations.

3.   I arrived at Leopoldville Airport about 4.30 on Monday 21st. I was met by Brigadier Otu. The situation on the airport was tense and we had considerable difficulty in getting Quarshie through the customs, which involved about one hour's delay. The head of the so-called Congolese Sûreté was extremely objectionable both to Quarshie and to me and I was to have difficulty with him later. The result of this delay was that I did not reach the United Nations building to see Rikhye until about six o'clock when it was beginning to get dark. On the way from the airport, Brigadier Otu explained to me the seriousness of the situation. He said that he was not sure whether Rikhye could restrain Mobutu's troops from attacking the embassy before I got there, and if Welbeck was not removed, serious fighting might break out. I explained to Otu my terms of reference from President Nkrumah, and he gave it as his opinion that they would be impossible to follow unless the United Nations as a whole were prepared to accept serious fighting and danger to the

lives of the Ghanaians other than Mr Welbeck. When I arrived at the United Nations building, Rikhye was in conference with the so-called Congolese Commissioners, trying to persuade them to restrain Mobutu until I arrived there. He apparently succeeded in getting an assurance from the latter that his troops would not attack before Quarshie and I had arrived.

While waiting to see Rikhye, I talked to his second-in-command, Quarshie and the operations officers (Indian), and came to the conclusion that unless blood was to be shed, the only choice was to remove Welbeck, if only temporarily. I therefore prepared a signal to this effect to the Ministry of Defence, for retransmitting to President Nkrumah. During the preparation of this signal, fighting broke out. I therefore added a sentence saying that I felt that the course I was about to adopt was the only one feasible under the circumstances.

I had a long discussion with Rikhye during which I explained my terms of reference which he considered were impossible to execute—i.e. he supported my views. I stated that I was quite prepared to try to get in to get Welbeck, provided Mobutu came with me to guarantee safe conduct. We made repeated telephone contact with Mobutu who refused to move. He said that he would organise the cease fire if I would guarantee that I would take Welbeck out of the country. As I had the Russian aircraft available I agreed to this, and in the end persuaded Mobutu to send two ANC officers to accompany me to the Residency. They took a long time to arrive and during this time I had repeated telephone messages from the Residency and spoke to both Welbeck and Mensah. Quarshie also had similar conversations with Welbeck. He asserted that unless we arrived within five minutes, he would be dead. I explained that I could not get in without safe conduct and was waiting for two Congolese officers to come with me. Eventually, I should think about 10.30 PM, the Congolese officers turned up. Quarshie, Rikhye and myself, with an escort of ANC and United Nations personnel, set off to try and get into the Residency. We made two attempts to get to his house but each time the firing increased and it was absolutely impossible to get into the embassy.

4.   During the time that Rikhye was negotiating with Mobutu (I refused to speak to Mobutu direct), I was spoken to by the

Tunisian ambassador, the commander of the Tunisian troops in Leopoldville, and the ambassador to the United Arab Republic. The Tunisian ambassador said that he was not prepared for more Tunisian troops to be killed in defence of Mr Welbeck and the Tunisian commander said the same thing very forcibly. They both considered it to be up to me to get Welbeck out as soon as I could get into him. The United Arab Republic ambassador said we must save Welbeck and stop the fighting.

5.   After failing in our attempt to get in to Welbeck, Rikhye and I, and, I think, Quarshie, went into the hospital to discover the extent of the casualties. The hospital itself was under fire. During my time there I saw eight wounded and two dead; one was Mobutu's second-in-command and another a Tunisian private. We then proceeded to Rikhye's house to discuss what to do next and rang up Welbeck, telling him that we could not rescue him that night and that I would try to do so at first light. At that stage I could not get Welbeck himself on the telephone but spoke to Mensah who said that the former was in his hideout. Rikhye undertook to continue negotiations with Mobutu and urge him to call a truce in order that I could get in. I then returned to my hotel. I left the hotel at 5.15 in the morning, after about two hours sleep, leaving Quarshie sleeping in his room because I did not consider it justifiable to expose him to any more danger. I proceeded to the United Nations operations room where I waited for Mobutu or a Congolese escort of some kind. While I waited there was desultory firing which gradually died down and I could see from the window of the operations room that a number of ANC were withdrawn from around the Ghana Residency. Eventually, at about 7.30, a Congolese officer (not Mobutu) and six other ranks arrived. They explained to me that they had come to give me safe conduct to the Residency and to the airport. I told them that I held them responsible for Welbeck's safe conduct to the airport, and obtained assurance from the officer that I could rely upon him. I then proceeded slowly to the Residency. By then there was scarcely a shot to be heard and very little sign of the ANC. On arrival at the Residency, I found the Tunisians still in position and that the officer commanding them had been wounded slightly in the head. I also spoke to several Ghanaian police who were severely shaken. We left the car on the road and I walked

into the Residency which did not appear to have suffered any damage. All the curtains were closed and the front room in darkness. I walked through to the bedroom wing and, in the darkened back room, found Welbeck and Mensah, sitting amongst their luggage. All I said to Welbeck was, 'Do you wish and are you ready to go?' He immediately replied, 'Yes, General', which was obvious from the fact that he was fully packed up and sitting waiting. I called in Captain Peel, the Ghana liaison officer in Leopoldville, and together we collected as much of the luggage as we could. The Tunisians gave us a hand in getting it to the cars. I did not show Welbeck President Nkrumah's letter to him for several reasons. First, I had forgotten to bring it from the hotel. Second, Welbeck had for the last thirteen hours been asking me to rescue him and it was quite obvious that no one—the Congolese, the Ghana police, the United Nations as a whole, Mensah and Welbeck himself—was prepared for him to stay any longer in the Residency. If he had, fighting would have broken out again, the Tunisians and the Ghana police would certainly have withdrawn and Welbeck and Mensah both have been killed.

6.   Third reason. At this stage, any action which might indicate that I was not prepared to fulfil the conditions of the truce would have led to wirespread fighting throughout Leopoldville, greatly endangering not only the Ghana police and civilians but all United Nations personnel in Leopoldville. I proceeded without incident to the airport where I was told by the head of the Sûreté that Quarshie had been arrested and must leave on the same aircraft as Welbeck. After having numerous arguments and varied insults hurled at me, I managed in the end to get the aircraft released after two hours. Had it not been for the great assistance given to me by the Tunisian officer at the Airport, I am certain that I myself would have been arrested. I did not accompany Welbeck because I wished to see Rikhye and Otu about the safety of the Ghana police and embassy staff still remaining in Leopoldville. I had lunch with Brigadier Otu who explained to me the extent of the anti-Ghana feeling which had been inflamed by the fact that Mobutu's second-in-command had been killed. After lunch I visited Rikhye, who said that it was in the interest of all that the evacuation of the police should now continue as previously agreed between the United Nations and the Ghana

government. He was concerned for my safety and offered me a helicopter to get to Brazzaville. He also expressed concern for the safety of the remaining embassy staff and the Ghanaian civilians. I left Leopoldville at about 4 PM.

7.   To sum up. I do not think I could have done anything but what I did under the circumstances, and in fact Welbeck signed a certificate willingly, saying that he was leaving at his own request to avoid bloodshed. It has been asserted that if Ghanaian troops had still been in Leopoldville, the situation need never have arisen. That is a matter of opinion, but it is quite certain that if Ghanaian troops had been involved in fighting, casualties would have been much heavier and the fighting much more difficult to stop. I had repeatedly pointed out earlier that as the United Nations were insisting upon the move of Ghanaian troops from Leopoldville, there were only two alternatives open to the Ghana government:

     1. to comply,
     2. to withdraw the Ghana army from the Congo.

B: A typical propaganda pamphlet from the Congo

SPECIAL BRANCH,
FORNUCO,
LEOPOLDVILLE (CONGO)
AUGUST 15, 1960.

English Version

Declaration made by 'La Jeunesse Populaire Africaine' (P.A.Y.) to the Press on Saturday, August 13, 1960, regarding the Republic of Congo

Dear Comrades and Friends,

The present difficult interim period in the Republic of the Congo necessitates reconciliation among all the Congolese.

When peril threatens at our doors, we must all fight it back. The union of every son of this country is an indispensable condition for safeguard. To be divided during the present moment is to encourage imperialist influence in our national territory. Sons and daughters of the country, who had lived in common and fought together against colonialism so as to regain their freedom, must be determinate in their revolution for a systematic transformation of their economic and social structure.

In view of the pressure of the situation, the 'Jeunesse Populaire Africaine', conscious of its patriotic duty and the ideal of making this country a strong and prosperous nation, deemed it good to stage the present demonstration. We are speaking to

137

every youth organisation, to our political leaders and, in particular, to our friends who support the acts of TSHOMBE, a smuggler in gold and copper under the leadership of the Belgian Imperialists. In the present circumstance, it is indispensable to be self-composed in order that the hatred expressed against the Government does not lead to vexatious consequences. The Office of TSHOMBE must be revoked and he himself must be arrested.

We invite all the Congolese to make all efforts for the reconstruction of our country through labour. We must expose the shame of those who are engaged in a race for power; and thereafter we shall realise peace and prosperity that we need. We have won the first victory of the struggle. Oh! it is a contraction; the colonial demagogues are using our brothers to establish the 'Divide and Rule' policy in order to perpetuate their benefits in our country. We have to tell those brothers that they are condemned by the world opinion. The most important order of the day is to fight for the territorial unity of all our forces in order to wipe out imperialist influence of whatever form. In the past, tribalism contributed a force for the failure of our national liberation. It must be denounced; for it is another form of racialism opposed to by the whole world. Its existence is always linked with and it constitutes a more dangerous type of colonialism than the type we have known since the 30th June. It is just the same as His Excellency the Prime Minister said that the eyes of the whole world were turned on to us.

Congo seriously needs changes. We must be the authors of those changes by our daily contribution to ease the task of the Central Government. The attainment of independence is the outcome of the revolution by the Congolese people in January, 1960, in which they still continue to indulge. No one can foil our right to freedom. Freedom is no synonym to assertion. There can be no freedom in a country where unemployment, troubles and misery prevail. We have confidence in our Government to take measures practicable to solve the situation. It depends upon ourselves to stay our economic independence and how to ensure a prosperous future. That is now the question for examination.

The Jeunesse Populaire Africaine jointly with others belonging to the Solidarity Group disapproves the attitude of the JABAKO which encourages the formation of the MUKONGO GOVERNMENT in haste. Let us expose the JABAKO of some anomalies which widely read: 'While the letter of the ABAKO to the House of the State of Leopoldville was in accordance with certain sections of the Constitution, some of our brothers had a different opinion. The telegram of the ABAKO to the Security Council declared that the people of MUKONGO were claiming federal Regime, while the Lower-River expressed the desire to maintain the integrity of the Leopoldville State; and for that much, they support the Central Government. The people of MUKONGO are a bit calm; our bitterness is self-explanatory, in that, we know that some members, for personal interests, and, who are opposed to the aims of the ABAKO, retained a defence counsel on behalf of the Party following the incident of the 4th January, 1959; and it was those same members who were attempting to lead Congo into misery. Yet they refused to allow themselves to be defended by a lawyer retained by the ABAKO.

Everyone knows very well that the present Government is practically incapable to make a programme at its investiture. Let us give the Government time to implement the belated programme, notwithstanding the difficulties prevailing.

Taking into consideration the present difficulties as the result of recent events, the Government should not be asked to submit a report on its activities just after one month of its investiture. To attack the Government at this period with the intention to vote it out is a pure folly and a proof of patriotic unconsciousness. If the Government commits errors, it is the duty of every citizen to suggest some solutions. This is the duty of a good citizen. It is not by incitement that the people will succeed in building up something real. Our action in this sense will prove our political immaturity to the whole world. While all the independent African Territories support our struggle against our former colonial masters, Congo goes divided. Frankly, we are discouraging the whole of Africa, and this is a shame. We are disrupting the efforts of all citizens towards the good management of the affairs of the country.

Conscious of his duty, the Jeunesses Populaire Africaine raises a solemn voice to point out to the Congolese people that the ambitious ignorant will be arraigned before the People's Tribunal, because they are victims for bargain at the profit of the imperialists for personal happiness.

The Jeunesse Populaire Africaine invites every Congolese

youth to place his country first. Let us unite to build together this new Congo.

Before the implementation of the Constitution, we will strongly oppose to splitting the country into bits; the result will lead the country into a disaster. We call upon the Provincial and the Central Governments to take measures against the abettors of these troubles by censuring them seriously. We cannot understand how members of a government constitutionally elected can sabotage its machinery by the endorsement of illegal documents.

The Belgian troops who are enemies to our independence, must leave our national territory. The Congolese people are peace loving. They cannot avenge the Belgians; for their acts have already exposed them to shame before the whole world.

We shall propose to the Government a general mobilisation of the youth. The volunteers will seek from recognised Governments of the Afro-Asian and Soviet countries military aid to drive away the Belgian troops from the Congo.

We shall co-operate with every country which is honest and co-operative; there must exist a mutuality. Those who have beaten us in the struggle for our freedom and the preservation of territorial integrity must know that although we have no fighting force, we will kick them out of our country.

Also, we shall call for the departure of Nationalist TCHANG-KAI-TCHECK's Chinese and the French Embassies who, by their commitments to the Security Council, have clearly manifested their co-operation with Belgium, our enemy.

We loudly raise our voice:

    'down with the imperialists, enemies to
      our independence and freedom;
    'long live the wise KASA-VUBU, Head of the
      State;
    'long live the Prime Minister, Patrice
      LUMUMBA;
    'long live the Jeunesse Populaire Africaine'.

The Council of the JPA
Leopoldville, 13/8/60.

C: A typical report written after a visit to the Congo

November 1960

Visit to the Congo—November 3–11

INTRODUCTION

1. The main purpose of my visit to the Congo was:
   a. To check the danger to the security situation in Leopold-ville, and in particular, to the safety of Mr Lumumba, which might result from the removal of Ghanaian Forces from the city.
   b. To visit Kasai, with a view to assessing the problem facing the Ghana Brigade in this large province, and give all the assistance I could to Brigadier Michel in carrying out his task.

LEOPOLDVILLE

2. As I have said in signals to Ghana, I am satisfied that the United Nations are firmly determined to protect the life of Mr Lumumba. On the other hand, I am not satisfied that the Tunisian contingent would be capable of keeping the security situation under control if the state of law and order deteriorates and I took the latter subject up with Brigadier Rikhye. He gave me an assurance that if such an eventuality did develop some Ghanaian troops would be flown back to Leopoldville. During my stay in Leopoldville I saw General Van Horn.

141

3. I am still of the view that, even if General Van Horn remains supreme commander, an experienced field military commander is needed to tackle the immense problem of restoring law and order throughout the Congo.

KASAI PROVINCE

4. During my visit to Kasai province I became appalled at the manner in which matters had deteriorated in all fields. I have touched on this in my various signals, but below I elaborate the main problems which I can only assume are typical to varying degrees throughout the Congo.

5. *Rival Factions.* The law and order problem is complicated by the emergence of rival interests. The main sections of the community competing for power are:

    a. The chiefs and their tribes.
    b. The administrators appointed by the central government at the time of independence.
    c. The Kalonjists.
    d. The Jeunesse.
    e. The Mining Company Forminière.
    f. The ANC.

In the middle of which is interposed a thin sprinkling of United Nations troops.

6. *The Chiefs and their Tribes.* First, to deal with the chiefs. At the latter part of their occupation the Belgians made endeavours to train political administrators, largely from Mr Lumumba's government and to cut down the power of the chiefs. This worked all right so long as Belgian military strength remained in the background, but once the Belgians and their military backing had gone, the chiefs' power started to rise and tribal warfare broke out all over the Congo. This warfare comes and goes according to the whims of the local chiefs and to the amount of authority which the United Nations are prepared to exert in any particular area.

Historically the 'aristocratic' tribes in Kasai province were mainly Lulua and Kinyoka. The Baluba held a very small area in Southern Kasai, their main strength lying in Katanga and Kivu. When the Belgians opened the mines in Kasai province and the missionaries penetrated the area, it was found that the Baluba were more willing to work and learn technical skills than the

142

aristocratic tribes. For this reason the mining companies imported the Baluba into mining areas and the latter gradually became more educated at the expense of the indigenous tribes, thereby taking over the more lucrative jobs in the mines themselves. Once the Belgians left, the Lulua and the Kinyoka worked together to massacre and eject the pockets of Baluba from the mining areas. Without this sprinkling of Baluba the mines cannot function properly. The chiefs themselves were happy to engage in tribal warfare whenever they thought they could be successful, but conversely they now have sufficient authority to bring peace to the tribes if they are prepared to do so.

7. *The Administrators.* The administrators are very young and very inexperienced. The majority are Lulua and they have not lost their tribal affiliations. Far from helping to bring peace to the tribes, there are many instances of their stirring up tribal hatred. This does not apply to the President of the province and some of his wiser councillors, but it certainly applies to those in outlying districts and the more irresponsible elements in Luluaburg.

8. *The Kalonjists.* The Kalonjists are a semi-trained army who support the break away of Southern Kasai from the central government at Leopoldville and Kalonji himself seems to sit in the safety of Brazzaville urging his men on from a distance. Whatever the Belgians may say, there is no doubt that this army has a number of ex-Belgian officers in it and, in fact, the army itself is led by a Belgian. The troops appear to be receiving modern weapons in increasing quantities and I can only assume that these are those taken from the Kamina Base at the time of the Belgians' departure. Day by day the situation regarding these troops becomes increasingly dangerous since they are ill-disciplined; part old Force Publique, and part ill-trained new recruits, equipped with highly efficient weapons.

9. *The Jeunesse.* The Jeunesse is a youth organisation being trained by NCOs from the Kalonjist army. Their training is very similar to that given to the Builders Brigade in this country except that many of them are armed with primitive weapons such as spears, bows and arrows and home-made guns. After a few weeks training the best of the Jeunesse are drafted into the Kalonjist army.

10. *Forminière.* It is difficult to be precise on the part being

played by the Forminière Mining Company. There is no doubt that unless law and order can be restored in Kasai, the few Belgian technicians in Kasai will leave and the mines close down, because the company itself cannot stand the financial loss indefinitely. On the other hand, it is my own view that, particularly in the Bakwakanga area, financial assistance to the Kalonjist army is being produced by Forminière. This view may be incorrect but it is certainly held by many people whom I met in Southern Kasai. It would seem to me that by far the wisest policy, both from the long term point of view, and for the mining companies and the Belgian technicians and settlers as a whole, is for the Kalonjists to withdraw to their bases, as have the ANC, and allow the United Nations to take over the responsibility for law and order. This, of course, presupposes that the United Nations are prepared to accept this responsibility and demand additional resources should these be necessary.

11. *ANC*. At present the ANC, after their original abortive attack on Katanga, are reasonably quiet but unless they can be given something constructive to do, they will not remain so indefinitely.

12. *The United Nations Forces*. The United Nations forces are thinly spread throughout the troubled areas of the province and, up to recently, have had neither the will nor the resources to restore law and order; but unless law and order are restored the economy of this province as a whole will soon disintegrate. The main task up to date assigned to the United Nations forces has been to keep the railway open. The railway is essential to the economy of Kasai. Without it the mines cannot operate and food cannot come into the province.

To sum up on the law and order situation: matters are really in a state of chaos, except in some areas where the United Nations troops are stationed, and even there trouble may break out again at any time. Without law and order the economy of the province can never be restored to normal, food cannot be distributed and starvation will reign.

13. *The Medical Problem*. The medical problem in Kasai as a whole is pathetic. Hardly any civilian doctors are left and practically all hospitals are closed. Disease and malnutrition are rampant.

14. *Food*. There is plenty of food in the province, if it could be distributed, but no one is prepared to go out of the main towns in

lorries to collect it for fear of being slaughtered. This accounts for the shortage of food in the main centres of population.

CONCLUSION

15. I came back from Kasai thoroughly depressed at the prospects of restoring life to normal in the Congo. The main weaknesses in the present United Nations effort appear to be as follows:

    a. *The lack of firm military direction.* It seems to me that the majority of those working at the United Nations headquarters in Leopoldville and the majority of the politicians in that city, who argue amongst themselves day by day, fail to realise what is happening outside Leopoldville: that the Congo is slowly but surely reverting to savagery and that unless the United Nations take a firm line, have adequate military resources at their disposal, and have adequate transport aircraft to move troops about, no one can save the Congo as a whole from complete economic collapse. For example, hardly any imports have come into Kasai province since July 9, practically all shops are shut and in Luluaburg alone, which is a small town, there are at least 40,000 unemployed.

    b. *Belgians.* It is quite obvious that the country will collapse unless some more Belgians return. It is the trader, administrator and technician type which are required. The United Nations should deport all Belgians who try to interfere with the internal politics of the country, which are complicated enough without interference from them.

16. I believe that the military resources available to the United Nations are still inadequate (much more so than before the situation deteriorated). The airlift is also inadequate. Politically, it seems very difficult to get the various powers to co-operate; but if this unhappy country is to be saved, all countries should be urged to co-operate, both financially and with military resources, in one last effort to restore law and order before political issues can be decided. If this were done, it would still be necessary to have experienced and firm military direction of a type acceptable to the contributing nations. I see no other hope for the Congo.

THE LESSON

17. The clear lessons to be drawn from the Congo would appear to be that:

    a. A Military Planning headquarters should be set up at UN headquarters in New York with resources at its disposal capable of intervening wherever necessary.

    b. The United Nations' first task must be to restore law and order in any operation of this kind. After all, the vast majority of the population in an undeveloped country of this nature are neither interested in nor affected by the higher political issues. All they want it to be able to live and work in peace, and the former administering power must obey the orders of, and co-operate with, the United Nations once the latter have been asked to intervene. It could well be that the final solution to the Congo problem is a loose federation, but in the long term it must be the Belgians themselves who will suffer if they think that the military support of secessionist movements is the best means of protecting their financial interests.

FOOTNOTE:

Since writing this report additional points have come to mind:

1. *Referendum.* Premier Lumumba's suggestion that there should be a referendum throughout the Congo is unrealistic. Under existing conditions it would be quite impossible to organise one.

2. *Conciliation Committee.* If this committee is to assess correctly the conditions in the Congo and make constructive, realistic suggestions towards a settlement, it must visit areas outside the main cities such as Leopoldville and Elizabethville.

3. *Katanga.* I do not know the accuracy of the reports that life is normal in Southern Katanga, i.e. about two-thirds of the Province. I know that this cannot be true in the extreme north, but am inclined to believe that conditions in Southern Katanga are reasonably normal, mainly because here there has been no clash between the ANC and Katanga forces.

D: A Cry from the Heart

'400 Cadets to Russia'

Colonel Arthur Ankrah,
1st Battalion, The Ghana Regiment of Infantry,
UN Forces, CONGO.

22nd September 1961

I am sorry that I have not written to you for some time but, as you are no doubt aware, life at the moment is by no means easy, and I am having rather a trying time. In many ways I wish you had been here to help, but from the few reports you sent us from the Congo there is no doubt that you are doing a first-class job of work and I congratulate you and those under your command. I hope you will pass these congratulations on.

There is one matter about which I feel I must in duty tell you. The President proposes to send 400 potential officers to the Soviet Union for training. I have done all I can to persuade him that such action is neither necessary nor prudent. It is not necessary because it will in no way speed up the rate of Africanisation which by doubling the size of the Academy I have already put at a gallop, and consider that by the end of next year the British contribution could without great danger be reduced to a training cadre. It is unwise for several reasons. Firstly, it splits the training and outlook of the Officers into two camps, and can breed neither contentment nor efficiency. Seondly, I consider that such action may in the long-term prove dangerous to the President himself. However, I have presented all these arguments, and many more. Nathan Afari has talked to him. Hassan has talked to him; all to no avail. I am not sure whether Steve has also spoken to the President about the matter but he may have, nor am I absolutely certain what Steve's own views are. But, to my mind, the main foolishness of the thing is that it is a risk that the President is taking which is quite unnecessary.

I felt that you ought to know this, and to be quite clear at the moment I am being tried very hard. I will do all I can to help the Ghana Army for so long as I can, but there is a limit under existing circumstances.

E: Letter of Dismissal from President Nkrumah

Ref No. SCR.0120

Accra.
22nd September 1961

Dear General,

I directed some time ago that you should make plans to turn the expatriate military personnel serving in Ghana into military missions. The purpose of this was to accelerate the Africanisation of the Armed Services.

I have also been greatly disturbed by the attitude which the British Government have taken over the question of Katanga in the Congo, and the assistance which the British Government have given to the secessionist elements in Katanga.

It is politically imperative that in present circumstances, direct command of the Ghana Armed Services should be held by Ghanaians, and I have decided that we must take a decisive step now for the complete Africanisation of the Armed Forces.

I will immediately assume the title of Supreme Commander of the Ghana Armed Forces. I have also decided to appoint Brigadier S. J. A. Otu, to be Army Chief of Staff in the rank of Major General Grade 1. I direct that you should hand over to Brigadier Otu forthwith the instruments of administration of the Ghana Armed Forces.

Yours sincerely,
KWAME NKRUMAH,
President.

Major General H. T. Alexander, CB, CBE, DSO,
Chief of Defence Staff,
Burma Camp, ACCRA.

Index of Names

151

Date Due

'77